DEER
STAND
DEVOTIONS

90 days on the hunt for God's direction in our lives

BY DEAN M. HULCE

Art provided by Dallen Lambson

Dallen's work can be seen and ordered at:
www.lambsonart.com
Lambson's Wildlife Art
1242 E. Alameda Rd.
Pocatello, ID 83201
1-800-756-4275

This Devotional Belongs to

_____

Psalm 96:11-12

Let the heavens rejoice, let the earth be glad; let the sea resound,
and all that is in it. Let the fields be jubilant, and everything in them;
let all the trees of the forest sing for joy.

DEDICATION PAGE

There are so many people that have an amazing impact on our lives. Some impact us in small ways some in big ways, some in our youth some later in life. God puts others around us that shape us.

As a boy I was surrounded by many godly men Mr. Kriegl, Mr. Kleiman, Mr. Willis, Pastor King, Darwin Wilson and many others. As I grew, God provided many friends who surrounded me and held me up. When I got married, Linda and I expanded our ring of friends. They were more of a blessing than we could have asked for. Some of those friends that sharpened us have been Paul and Norma, Donna and Ron, Tom and Laura, Brandt and Kelli, Doug and Sue, Dan, Tim and many more. All of you are loved more than you know.

Growing up, with 5 boys and one girl, we lived through the good, the bad and the ugly. Dave, Dan, Dale and Daryl, thank you for true brotherhood. Becky, thank you for loving everyone no matter what, you were taken too young but we will see you again soon. Mom, you made our house a home like no one could have done and despite a few broken wooden spoons you always cared for each of our needs. Dad, you too went way too soon, but when you were here you taught me the value of hard work and hard hunting and I never doubted your love.

Our family means the world to me. Micah, Chloe, Harli and Hunter I love you very much. Ryan and Nick, you guys have driven me to be better, a better father and a better person. Linda, you are my best friend. When people kiddingly talk about our better halves... that would be you for me. I love you more than life itself. Thank you for always believing in me and supporting me.

Steve Mairs, thirty years has flown by. Our friendship has been through so much. I appreciate and love you like another father. Thank you!

A very special thank you to Jim, Randy, Jim and Scott from Trophies of Grace Ministries in Wisconsin and Florida and John from The Legacy Group of America. Without you all this would not be possible.

Jesus is who I depend on above all others. I am who I am because of Him.

A Special Thank You To My Supporting Ministry Partners

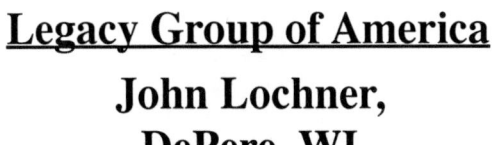

Legacy Group of America
John Lochner,
DePere, WI

Trophies of Grace
Northern Division
Jim and Helen Panetti
Randy Malcore,
Green Bay, WI

Trophies of Grace
Southern Division
Jim, Scott and Mark Porter,
Molino, FL

FORWARD

W hat a privilege and an honor to be asked by Dean Hulce to write the forward to his new book *Deer Stand Devotions*. I have to admit, when first approached I asked him "why me?" What qualifies me to write anything about anybody, let alone something about the author for his new book?

Looking back on my 20+ year friendship with Dean it occurred to me how influential and spiritually guiding he has been throughout this time. Together we have spent many hours in the vehicle together. We laugh and joke but many times our conversations turn to spiritual questions, usually put forth by me.

I have learned that Dean will usually listen carefully, not jump to any quick conclusions and then answer my questions thoughtfully, and with no judgment. It is very similar to how his daily devotionals have guided me, and I am sure many of you, for awhile now. It seems that just about the time I may be having thoughts or questions, or maybe something is not going quite right in my life at the time, I will read one of Dean's devotionals or short stories and things just fall back into perspective.

The positive messages received on a daily basis through Dean's devotionals have helped me, and I am sure many of you, become better people. Recently Dean wrote a piece based on Proverbs 17:22 "A joyful heart is good medicine, but a crushed spirit dries up the bones." He went on to share a story of keeping joy in your life no matter the situation and how we should all prioritize life. It went like this:

JOY = Jesus > Others > Yourself

Dean summed it up with, "The key to Joy is counting our own desires or our own wants and needs less than those of others and even more so, less than our desire for Jesus and the direction that He has for us." – PERFECT!

Enjoy the enclosed messages and see if they do not apply to your own life in many ways. Reread them at different times throughout the year and find new meanings that will apply to your own spiritual journey.
Thank you Dean for sharing with all of us and for helping to keep Joy in our lives!

Dan Diesler

SPIRITUAL NUTRITION

Psalm 23:1-3 (NIV)
1 The Lord is my shepherd, I want for nothing. 2 He makes me lie down in green pastures, he leads me beside quiet waters, 3 He refreshes my soul. He guides me along the right paths for His name's sake.

E very good land manager knows that the deer on his or her property need green foods. The shepherds of the Bible times knew this same thing about their sheep. They understood that the sheep needed good nutritious feed to thrive.

Deer hunters today know that wildlife doesn't just need good nourishing food during the hunting season, but year round. If the bucks are going to be healthy and grow large antlers, they will need protein in large quantities as well as other minerals. Does as well need the right nutrition to help produce what they need to nurse their young and still have enough energy to retain good condition.

Christians today need an adequate amount of spiritual nutrition to not only grow, but to just survive in our world today. Christians are not thriving and multiplying God's family, because we are not healthy. We're lacking the spiritual nutrition that allows us to be as healthy as possible.

God's people have not been going to the "green pastures" of God's Word to get the nutrition they need to grow, thrive and multiply. Like a female deer that is too weak to produce the next generation, a Christian that is not fed high quality spiritual food will not be spiritually strong enough to produce the next generation within God's family.

There is a difference between the Christian not getting what they need to grow and a deer or deer herd lacking in nutrition. God's people have a constant supply of spiritual nourishment while the deer will go through times of stress when there is no quality food. All of us have access to God's Word, the Bible, on your desktop, computer, laptop, tablet or phone. There is a never ending supply; all we have to do is to consume it on a regular basis. There are so many things in life that would be much easier if we relied on God's supply of high quality nutrition.

Christians, live to your fullest potential by being consistent students of the God's Word, the Bible. Biblical nutrition will help you stand strong and defeat the devil throughout your life all the while giving God the Glory.

SET APART

1 Peter 2:9

But you are a chosen race, a royal priesthood, a holy nation, a people for his own possession, that you may proclaim the Excellencies of him who called you out of darkness into his marvelous light.

Yesterday morning I was blessed with the chance of a lifetime... Linda and I were hunting deer in South Dakota with great friends. In the area we were hunting others had been seeing a drop tine whitetail and I was hoping to bump into him. The first morning of the season was great, with deer moving all around. Two hours after daylight the drop tine buck showed up and I was so blessed to harvest him. So what? For most deer hunters a buck with drop tine antlers is a type of "Holy Grail". These deer are estimated to be one in a thousand. They truly are "set apart" in the world of trophy bucks.

Those of us that are Christians are "set apart" from the rest of the world. We are, as Peter said it, "a royal priesthood." How many of us live up to this title in life. When the world sees us, do we look like we are different and a part of God's family? Or can they not see anything special in us? Are we like everyone else or are we seen as just "one of the guys or girls." We need to be "in this world but not of this world."

The apostle Paul declared himself, "special" in Romans 1:1, when he introduced himself as, "Paul, a servant of Christ Jesus, called to be an apostle, set apart for the gospel of God."

Are you just a "typical" worldly person, or are you set apart as a trophy for your Lord?

Be set apart.

I KEEP FALLING IN LOVE WITH HIM

Acts 4:31
And when they had prayed, the place where they had gathered together was shaken, and they were all filled with the Holy Spirit and began to speak the word of God with boldness.

There's nothing like a fresh morning in the mountains. The air feels so great as you take a deep breath and it clears your lungs and somehow seems to clear your mind. That is what the Holy Spirit can do for us. He can work to completely fill us and refresh us.

D.L. Moody said it this way...
"You might as well try to see without eyes, hear without ears, or breathe without lungs, as to try to live the Christian life without the Holy Spirit."

There's an old hymn that explains what happens when we're filled with the Holy Spirit...

I keep falling in love with Him
Over and over and over and over again

He gets sweeter and sweeter as the days go by
Oh what a love between my Lord and I
I keep falling in love with Him
Over and over and, over and over again

As we fall deeper in love with God, our entire life changes.

Act 1:8 "But ye shall receive power, after that the Holy Ghost is come upon you: and ye shall be witnesses unto me both in Jerusalem, and in all Judaea, and in Samaria, and unto the uttermost part of the earth."

_____

_____

_____

_____

_____

SPEAKING WELL

James 3:3-6

If we put bits into horses' mouths to make them obey us, we can guide their whole bodies as well. 4 And look at ships! They are so big that it takes strong winds to drive them, yet they are steered by a tiny rudder wherever the helmsman directs. 5 In the same way, the tongue is a small part of the body, yet it can boast of great achievements. A huge forest can be set on fire by a little flame. 6 The tongue is a fire, a world of evil. Placed among the parts of our bodies, the tongue contaminates the whole body and sets on fire the course of life, and is itself set on fire by hell.

There isn't much that I enjoy more in the outdoors than calling elk, deer and turkeys; talking to animals and getting them in close. One time in the mountains of North Central Colorado I had a good bull elk coming my way when I tried to make one more call to "finish the deal". The sound that came out of the call was nothing like the one that was in my head and it ended the hunt short. Instead of speaking well, I used the call in a bad way.

How often we catch ourselves speaking badly of someone when we could have just as easily spoken positively or said nothing at all. We are given the ability to speak and the freedom to use this ability, yet we so often abuse it.

When we learn to hold our tongue or speak blessings we will find that we receive blessing as well.

Start practicing uplifting speech and verbal blessings... We will be amazed at how it will change our lives.

THERE'S POWER IN THE BLOOD

Hebrews 9:22
In fact under the Law almost everything is purified by means of blood, and without the shedding of blood there is neither forgiveness for sin.

To all of my friends it would come as no surprise that I love to hunt... I've spent much of my life hunting or more so taking others hunting. One of my favorite things to do in hunting is trailing/tracking an animal to harvest. A good "blood trail" is an exciting thing. The blood is what brings life to the animal. The "heavier" the trail the better chance for success... WITHOUT BLOOD THERE IS NO LIFE. Any hunter can relate to this.

More than anything else in the body, blood is essential to life. It's what carries the fuel and oxygen to the billions of cells in our bodies. Blood supplies the brain and the heart with the necessary nourishment to function. It also carries carbon dioxide and other waste materials to the correct system, where they are then removed from the body. Without blood we couldn't keep warm or cool, fight infections, or get rid of our own waste products. Additionally, our very identity, our DNA, is located in our blood.

We must understand this: God is so obsessed with blood because He's so obsessed with life not death. The Israelites while in Egypt put the blood of a pure lamb on their door posts to preserve their life. They also sacrificed pure animals, by shedding the blood, to receive forgiveness for their sins.

Thank God that today we don't have to do that. Jesus came and gave of himself so that we are cleansed by His blood. Christ's blood was shed to bring us life... He came for that purpose. Death didn't hold Him.

Romans 5:10
For if, while we were God's enemies, we were reconciled to him through the death of his Son, how much more, having been reconciled, shall we be saved through his life!

PUTTING OFF THE OLD

Ephesians 4:22-24 (NIV)
22 You were taught, with regard to your former way of life, to put off your old self, which is being corrupted by its deceitful desires; 23 to be made new in the attitude of your minds; 24 and to put on the new self, created to be like God in true righteousness and holiness.

We just got back from a trip across the southern states. In Texas, while we were turkey hunting, we saw whitetail bucks without antlers and some still carrying their racks. Most bucks and bull elk across the country have dropped their antlers by this time of the year or are in the process.

Shedding antlers is very similar to what should happen to the children of God. When antlers shed it is removing old dead weight and replacing it with new living tissue. If the old antlers didn't fall off there would be no possibility of the new healthy, quite often bigger and stronger, antlers to grow.

If a Christian doesn't get rid of the sinful past, there is no room for the new way of life. No matter how much we try to change and grow it just can't happen. Until the old is gone, the growth of the new is impossible.

In 2 Corinthians, Paul writes that "Christians are a new creation..." Not just changed, but new.

2 Corinthians 5:17(NKJV)
Therefore, if anyone is in Christ, he is a new creation; old things have passed away; behold, all things have become new.

So if you haven't gotten rid of the old, do that or new growth can't happen. You are a new creation.

_____

_____

_____

_____

_____

NO PROBLEM TOO BIG

Jeremiah 32:17
"Ah Lord GOD, behold, thou hast made the heaven and the earth by thy great power and stretched out arm, and there is nothing too hard for thee:"

I was driving in a pouring rain, racing back from a storm on the mountain. The water was running like thin pudding down the road, but so far my tires were holding to the mud. Just before heading downhill toward camp, I went through a twenty-yard-long dip in the road. As I tried to come out of it, my tires started to not only spin but slide sideways as well. Two more feet and my truck, along with Harris and I, were going over the edge. I stopped and got out through the passenger's side. We called for a ride and then got a come-along cable and attached my truck to the closest tree uphill. I fear that without that cable the truck would have gone over the edge and been destroyed.

Life is quite often like that, and when we feel as though there is no way through our trouble and strife, we need to remember this verse. If He made the heavens and the Earth, then *He* certainly controls it. "And there is nothing too hard for thee." God is the cable that keeps us from disaster.

Why do we ever doubt that God, in his infinite wisdom, couldn't handle a problem that is fairly meaningless in the face of eternity?

Maybe God is just waiting for us to fully surrender to His will for us.

19

SEEK YE FIRST

Exodus 20:1-3 (ESV)
"And God spoke all these words, saying, 'I am the Lord your God, who brought you out of the land of Egypt, out of the house of slavery. You shall have no other gods before me.' "

I remember one Sunday morning when I was a teenager, my brothers and I were walking along a small dirt road on our way back to camp during deer season. A pickup truck pulled up alongside of us and Angelo Chiocchi, an older local man, rolled down his window and asked, "Where's your dad this morning?"

We answered, "He's in church."

To that Angelo laughed and said, "Your dad is the only man I know that can kill a buck while sitting in a pew." And he drove away still laughing. That was forty years ago, but it has stuck with me. I'm not sure what the rest of us were doing out of church that morning, but dad was there.

I've had so many people tell me that they don't need to go to a church because they worship in their boat or in the woods. While I agree that worshipping in these places can be a great time with God, when we allow our passion to take first place it becomes a problem.

I've known people who love their jobs and they truly find their importance in their work. Like hunting, fishing or any other hobby, there is nothing wrong with loving your job, however, when we quit working to live and start living to work, again we have a problem. When our work, passion, family, hobbies or anything else gets in the way of our relationship with God, we have a *big problem*—a sin problem. We are allowing other things to take God's place in our lives.

I'm not suggesting that you can't miss church to be hunting or fishing with your family or friends. What I am saying is when we forget where our importance comes from, God, and start making other things more important than Him, we are out of line. In the book of Matthew, Jesus said something about our desires that should effect what we keep number one in our lives.

"But seek first the kingdom of God and his righteousness, and all these things will be added to you" (Matthew 6:33, (ESV).

Keep God first and He will supply the rest.

WHERE YOUR TREASURE IS

Luke 12:32-34
32 "Do not be afraid, for your Father has been pleased to give you the kingdom. 33 Sell your possessions and give to the poor. Provide purses for yourselves that will not wear out, a treasure in heaven that will never fail, where no thief comes near and no moth destroys. 34 For where your treasure is, there your heart will be also.

I have progressed over the years from a hunting fanatic to a scouting and guiding fanatic. I love to sit for hours staring at maps on my computer. I also love to discover new places to hunt or more likely to set someone else up to hunt. I could do this for weeks on end. I enjoy this to the point where I lose sleep over it, sometimes day after day. It sometimes becomes obsessive.

Fall is here, I want to spend every waking hour "seeing what's over the next hill." Now I have to question how much I love/treasure this desire. Is this where my true treasure is?

We all have things in our lives that we treasure: relationships, possessions, hobbies etc... Whatever it might be, we need to make sure that what we treasure more than anything on earth is the Lord. No matter how good something is, we need to ALWAYS keep God first in everything!

YOU ARE SIGNIFICANT

Psalms 34:17-20

17 The righteous cry out, and the Lord hears them; he delivers them from all their troubles. 18 The Lord is close to the brokenhearted and saves those who are crushed in spirit. 19 The righteous person may have many troubles, but the Lord delivers him from them all; 20 he protects all his bones, not one of them will be broken.

In the Fish Lake National Forest in Utah there is a colony of quaking aspen, known as Pando, or the Trembling Giant. On the western edge of the Colorado Plateau this single root system has been alive for unknown years, possibly since Noah's flood.

Taken as a whole, all the individual trunks, branches and leaves weigh in at an estimated 6,600 tons: The heaviest known organism on the planet. And it's a tree, or, rather, trees, larger than any other plant and certainly any animal, covering 106 acres. It's a single organism, sometimes being driven back by fire above ground but remaining alive below. It's just a single root system below ground that connects thousands upon thousands of aspen trees above.

Now consider that this enormous organism is tiny compared to our world, much smaller yet than the Milky Way, our Galaxy and the Milky Way is only a miniscule dot in the face of the universe. There are other galaxies that are many times larger (150+) than our Galaxy and there are millions of galaxies that are millions of mile apart...

Do you feel tiny and insignificant yet? Well don't! As small as we are in stature compared to all of God's creation, realize this... It was just for you that the same powerful God gave up His own son to die. Now that is important!

Romans 5:8

But God commanded His love towards us, in that, while we were yet sinners, Christ died for us

You are significant!

OLD SIGNS

Psalm 71:18 (ESV)
18 So even to old age and gray hairs, O God, do not forsake me, until I proclaim your might to another generation, your power to all those to come.

The property that we hunted as kids had old wooden tree stands all over. Wherever we found a good place to hunt we would build another stand. There were wooden steps hanging at different angles everywhere.

Now when I lease a new piece of land, I look for old stands that people built years ago, wooden skeletons hanging in old trees. These same places are good indicators of quality locations from days gone by that also may still be the right places today. They are like old road signs that point out the right way.

As we go through life we encounter older people that show us the good things in life. Today we call them, mentors. These people have lived through the things that we will face in the future. They have built lives through experience. We need to align ourselves with the hearts of those that are experienced in a godly life, those that God has shown His way in this world. These men and women have the wisdom that God has given them through years of trials.

These are the signs set before us... Signs of wisdom and experience that God has used as guide posts from one generation to the next.

And as we get older then we have a responsibility ourselves to pass that same God given wisdom to the next generations.

Bernard Kelvin Clive explains it this way, "Mentorship is simply learning from the mistakes and mastery of a successful person..."

Proverbs 27:17
As iron sharpens iron, so one man sharpens another.

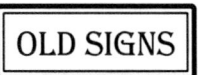

_____

_____

_____

_____

IN SEASON AND OUT

2 Timothy 4:2
Preach the word; be prepared in season and out of season; correct, rebuke and encourage—with great patience and careful instruction.

As hunters we all know of the armies of guys that pull into an area the night before season and hunt a few days and go back home, generally without success. Then there are those of us that live the hunt year round. If we aren't hunting we're studying maps, hanging stands, searching for shed antlers etc... It is a yearlong endeavor. We're all in.

If we were all in for Him, can you imagine how God could use us if our spiritual life was as intense as our hunting or fishing life? If we were "prepared in season and out of season", imagine what God could do through each of us.

God probably isn't going to call you to leave the outdoors, but He might. More likely God is calling you to give Him more passion, more dedication and more love for Him and His work than you do for anything and everything else in your life.

In Psalm 37:4 the writer tells us this...
Delight thyself also in the Lord: and he shall give thee the desires of thine heart.

There's a great promise in that verse. If we delight in the Lord, He will give us the desires of our heart. When our hearts align with His, our desires become His desires. Go all in.

_____

_____

_____

_____

_____

_____

_____

PROVISION OF WATER

Psalm 104:10
He makes springs pour water into the ravines; it flows between the mountains.

P salm 104:6-16 speaks of God's awesome provision of water. He spoke and the waters listened. Every life on earth is dependent on earthly water to survive... And the Lord provides it in His timing.

If you have ever driven through parts of Kansas, Nebraska, Oklahoma and Texas in a period of drought you know what it is like to "need" water. The plants are either gone or stressed. Even the antlers of the deer are stunted from the need for water. In the worst of conditions the animals perish.

In the midst of mankind's drought, Christ came as "Living Water." Our souls cannot "survive" without this living water. Once we've trusted Christ to be our source of life, then God's word becomes our "water" and "food" so we continue to keep growing.

Without water and food we eventually weaken and die... Daily food and water is required. Don't let your spiritual life go dormant, feed and water it daily with God's word and with prayer.

BLIND FAITH

John 20:28-29
28 Thomas answered and said to Him, "My Lord and my God!" 29 Jesus said to him, "Because you have seen Me, have you believed? Blessed are they who did not see, and yet believed."

G ood hunters are a faithful bunch. They will sit for days waiting in one spot hoping that their prey will come by. There was a time, and it wasn't too many generations back, where it was a matter of life and death. If you didn't harvest an animal, you didn't eat meat for a while. Today it's different. We don't have to count on game meat to survive. We also don't have to wonder if game is in or travels through our area. Some hunters use feeders & trail cameras, which will capture photos & video of the animals and their habits and send them to their phone. There isn't a big need for a great amount of faith in most hunting these days.

The day after Christ's resurrection He appeared to the disciples. According to John's account, Thomas wasn't present at first and didn't believe it was really the Messiah that the others were seeing. He needed proof. I can't say that I would have had more faith than Thomas.

The Christian life, as in hunting, requires a great deal of faith and trust. We can either doubt that He will come through when we need Him or we can wait patiently for Christ to show us He is real and we can count on Him.

Don't be a doubting Thomas. Trust that Christ is real and is always there beside His children. We don't need to see Him, we can see what He does and how He works.

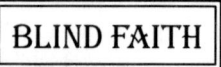

_____

_____

_____

_____

_____

_____

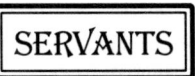

SERVANTS

John 13:12-17 (KJV)

12 So after he had washed their feet, and had taken his garments, and was set down again, he said unto them, do you know what I have done to you? 13 You call me Master and Lord: and you say well; for so I am. 14 If I then, your Lord and Master, have washed your feet; you also ought to wash one another's feet. 15 For I have given you an example, that you should do as I have done to you. 16 Verily, verily, I say unto you, The servant is not greater than his lord; neither he that is sent greater than he that sent him. 17 If you know these things, happy are you if you do them.

I had a great friend that was a humble servant. He had a passion to take others hunting. Curtis lived to share the outdoors with those that needed his help. If there was a season open, he was in the woods quite often with a child or somebody else that either needed a place to hunt or someone to show them how it was done. He gave up of his own time and put aside his desire to harvest and animal for the wants and needs of others.

I learned a lot from Curtis, but mostly I learned that when given a gift, we need to share it. Today we call it, "paying it forward." In Christ's day, it was called, "being Christ-like." We need today to be like Curtis or more appropriately, Christ-like in how we serve others.

The day before Christ's crucifixion was when the Last Supper was eaten and the evening when Christ washed the feet of His disciples. We need to learn from His example and do the job of the servant. Washing the feet of guests was just that, the job of a servant. If that job was good enough for Christ, it should be good enough for us.

We need to leave our own desires and egos at the door and put ourselves in the place of service to show the love of Christ.

ONLY WHATS DONE FOR CHRIST

James 4:14 (NIV)
Why, you do not even know what will happen tomorrow. What is your life?
You are a mist that appears for a little while and then vanishes.

When I shot my first whitetail buck I was 15 years old and I asked my dad if I could have it mounted. While it was just an average sized 7 point buck, at that time my dad saw no value in mounting any whitetail, let alone an average buck.

Since that time my family has had many trophies go to the taxidermist and come home to our walls. For a long time I thought that these mounts would always hold a prestigious place in our home or camp. But as time has passed some of those memories have begun to fade and the "value" of some of the mounts has lessened in my eyes.

One of the things that we have to realize is that life goes by so fast and all of the "things" that we have felt are important really don't have eternal value.

There is an old saying, "Only one life, 'twill soon be past, only what's done for Christ will last."

For those that know Christ, the rest of the business of life gets in the way of serving and living for Him. Those things that fade with time take away from those things that are really important.

What's important to you? Where is your passion? Are you living your passion for Christ? Everything will soon pass away and all the trophies and other things of this world will have no value...

Hold on to this... "Only what's done for Christ will last"

_____

_____

_____

_____

_____

PROTECT YOUR HEART

1 Corinthians 15:33(NLT)
Don't be fooled by those who say such things, for "bad company corrupts good character."

In most of the country there is a special time of the year for deer hunters. It happens right around the first two weeks of November. This is the "magic" time for harvesting whitetail bucks. Why?

At about that time each year the female deer start to cycle so they are ready and willing to breed. Bucks that are generally extremely secretive and spooky all of a sudden allow their guard to be let down and travel all hours of the day and night in cover and in the open.

We are like those bucks... We can live a good clean godly life for long periods of time, and then we will allow someone or something to pull us out from under the safety of our close daily walk with the Lord. One day, like those trophy bucks, we find ourselves in trouble. Remain on that path with God, not veering off and allowing yourself to be drawn away.

When I was in high school I heard pastor Nick Scroggins say, "If you take a white glove and throw it into a mud puddle, don't expect the puddle to turn white, expect the glove to get dirty."

Protect your heart, stay close to God, always.

_____

_____

_____

_____

_____

_____

_____

STRONG FENCES

Colossians 1:23 (KJV)

If ye continue in the faith grounded and settled, and be not moved away from the hope of the gospel, which ye have heard, and which was preached to every creature which is under heaven; whereof I Paul am made a minister;

I f you were to set out to build a straight fence you wouldn't be haphazardly setting poles in the ground without direction. You would dig one deep hole first to securely hold your post. Then as each post goes in you look back down the line of posts to make sure that they line up straight. Each post, like the first is buried deep to make sure it has a firm foundation, grounded well, and then it has solid dirt or gravel packed around it to keep it from wavering back and forth.

As children of God we need to be well grounded on a firm foundation of faith and then be set in place by study of God's word so as not to waiver when pressures come against us.

If a fence is not secure it will topple over the first time that something applies pressure to it. It also is strengthened and tightened by being well connected to other fence posts of similar strength.

So it goes for God's people... We need to be bound to others with similar beliefs and strengths. We then are held up by those around us that are in turn held up by us.

God's family, if it's to be strong, needs to be like a strong, straight fence. Holding each other up when the pressures of life push in on us.

Thank you to all of you like-minded fence posts that hold me up.

HE DOES THE IMPOSSIBLE... ALL THE TIME

Jeremiah 18:14
Does the snow of Lebanon ever vanish from its rocky slopes?
Do its cool waters from distant sources ever stop flowing?

O ur God is a God of wonders. Who can really understand how our world or our universe works? We hear fools try to explain how or why certain things within our world do what they do... But I don't think we can answer the question, why.

There are rivers in the mountains that if you follow them to their source, you will find water pouring out of a rock... Not just any rock, but a rock at 12,000 ft + in elevation. There is no normal water table at that elevation, no snow pack above it to melt down into the rocks. To the human mind this cannot happen.

I took a friend to see this a year ago; this friend runs a water system for a small town. We drove up to a place where we could use our binoculars to glass to the water springing from the rocks. His words were, "that isn't possible." To the human mind it is impossible, but to God this is like child's play.

I love having a relationship with a God who is in the business of doing the impossible. It gives me hope every day.

Are you trusting in a God that can make water come from a broken rock or are you trusting in your own abilities?

The same thing happened in the dessert with Moses and his staff. Numbers 20:11 (NIV) Then Moses raised his arm and struck the rock twice with his staff. Water gushed out, and the community and their livestock drank.

Where is your hope?

HE>I – HE GREATER THAN I

John 3:30 (KJV)
He must increase, but I must decrease.

Tonight I walked past a pickup truck that had a sticker on the back window that said this, "HE>I". It took me a minute to figure it out. What an amazing three letters and symbol. In grade school math that might have read, "He is greater than I."

At the time the words from John 3:30 were spoken, there were few that had reason to be proud of their work for God. John the Baptist was one that might have had something to boast in, yet his concern was that he decrease in stature and Christ be elevated.

In order for you and me to show Christ to others in an effective way, we have to allow God to grow in importance in our hearts, minds and lives. For myself, I pray that God will continually work on me to break my pride.

I think of it as a large tree being chewed by a beaver. Each day that beaver goes back. Day after day he chips out one little piece of wood after another. One day that tree will fall and I hope that my pride, my self-importance, my life will follow like that tree, totally broken off.

Lord, I pray that our lives will be filled with a desire to elevate you to the world around us and never a desire to elevate ourselves.

May HE always be > than I.

_____

_____

_____

_____

_____

_____

HOW GREAT IS OUR GOD?

Psalm 14:1 (KJV)
The fool hath said in his heart," There is no God. They are corrupt, they have done abominable works, there is none that doeth good.

R ecently I spent a day at the Creation Museum in Kentucky... What an eye opener! I know what I believe and I have no doubts, however, yesterday taught me some amazing facts about why I believe what I believe.

If scientists really looked at the proof of creation with an open mind, they would have to question secular science theories.

Did you know that the sun is shrinking at a rate that if the earth was really millions of years old, the sun would have been so big the heat would have made the earth uninhabitable? Were you aware that a huge canyon was formed by the runoff of Mount Saint Helen and that scientist normally would have claimed it had taken millions of years? But they saw it happen in days, not centuries.

Dr. Louis Bounoure, a prominent Swiss scientist, summed it up rather succinctly when he stated in The Signs of Nature, "Evolution is a fairy tale for grownups! The theory has helped nothing in the progress of science. It is useless." The truth is that science disproves any theory of a slowly evolving earth, again confirming special creation.

There are countless signs that show us that life was created, it didn't just happen. We need to become familiar with God's truths so we can stand for God in the midst of the world views.

THE PATHS WE CHOOSE

Proverbs 4:25-27 (KJV)

25 Let thine eyes look right on, and let thine eyelids look straight before thee. 26 Ponder the path of thy feet, and let all thy ways be established. 27 Turn not to the right hand nor to the left: remove thy foot from evil.

One of the best afternoon hunts on the Cielo Vista Ranch is a walk that comes off of The Crow's Nest on Spencer Mountain, down across Perdido Creek and down the Bernadito Trail which runs alongside Bernadito Creek. It is a rare afternoon that you are not close to elk all afternoon. The problem with this hunt is that it is too good at times and the last 1/2 mile can be treacherous. When the hunting is good, you come off the mountain in the dark. The path is steep and washed out in places. The footing is secure, but only if you keep your eyes directly on the path and you have something to illuminate your way. I had one night in particular that I wasn't sure I was getting back to the truck with all my limbs intact. It had been a long night and I only had a small light.

Life is just like the descent down Bernadito Trail. If we allow God to lead us and we remain in His light we will make it through safely, however if we take our eyes off of the path He has laid out for us, or we decide to walk out in the darkness we will surely stumble and quite often fall.

Throughout the Bible, God promises to take care of us, if we hold tight to His path. Once we've known the comfort and safety of a life close to Christ, why would we want to do anything else?

John 15:7 (KJV)

If ye abide in me, and my words abide in you, ye shall ask what ye will, and it shall be done unto you.

Keep your eyes on His path.

_____

_____

_____

_____

WHERE IS YOUR DELIGHT

Psalm 119:143
Trouble and distress have come upon me,
but your commands give me delight.

I find it funny that David writes that trouble and distress have "come upon me"... We don't have to go looking for trouble; it will come to us without looking for it. We double our *"trouble and distress"* when we move away from the Lord and dabble on the edge of sin.

Romans 6:6, tells us, "We should no longer be slaves to sin,"

Charles Spurgeon wrote about this... "Dear Christian, why are you flirting with sin? Hasn't it cost you enough already? Will you continue to play with fire even after you've been burned? After having been caught in the jaws of the lion, will you now step a second time into his den? Don't be so foolish."

I've always wondered how, in the world of hunting, that poachers found any enjoyment, any pride in taking an illegal animal. How do they brag about a trophy or thrill in the harvest of any animal? I can't imagine delighting in anything that was done illegally.

There is an old saying, "they are good who delight in good things, and they are evil who delight in evil things."

Where is your delight today?

_____

_____

_____

_____

_____

_____

_____

ARMED PREY

James 4:7-8(NASB)
7 Submit therefore to God. Resist the devil and he will flee from you. 8 Draw near to God and He will draw near to you. Cleanse your hands, you sinners; and purify your hearts, you double-minded.

I live in an area that is highly populated with porcupines. In the spring you see them taking a permanent "nap" next to the road. Porcupines are very interesting creatures in that they are relatively slow and docile, but get too close and you will see them become defensive in a hurry. Dogs that are unfamiliar with a porcupine's defenses often get themselves in a great deal of trouble, resulting in a far greater deal of pain. Wild predators know better.

I remember a saying that went like this, "When the prey is armed, the enemy thinks twice." This is true of porcupines in the wild but is never truer than in our lives.

In the second part of verse seven above it says, "Resist the devil and he will flee from you." This shows that if we are armed with God's word, presence, peace and God's Son… the devil will flee from us. We are the "armed prey."

We can come under attack by Satan when we are children of God but if we are spending serious time in His word and are drawn near to Him in prayer on a regular basis, Satan knows it. When the attack comes, stick even closer to God and demand that Satan get away from you. Resist him and he will leave.

Arm yourself with the things of God and resist the devil and he will flee from you.

_____

_____

_____

_____

_____

_____

BUCK FEVER

Romans 8:9
"You, however, are controlled not by the sinful nature but by the Spirit, if the Spirit of God lives in you. And if anyone does not have the Spirit of Christ, he does not belong to Christ".

There's a strange ailment that falls on men, women and children of ages old enough to hunt. I've seen it take grown men that are as strong as an ox and turn them into Jello. Men have been known to draw their bows and hold at full draw while a bull elk walks by at under 20 yards and then do it again when the bull is called back past, forgetting the whole time to release the arrow.

This ailment is known as "Buck Fever." Most everyone that hunts has some level of this debilitating sickness at one time or another. It generally leaves you sick to your stomach, babbling incoherently, shaking uncontrollably and with an inability to stand.

Nevertheless, as powerful as "buck fever" is, there is something much stronger at work in us. This power occasionally erupts and injures anyone that is close to us. The power that I am talking about doesn't just affect hunters but unfortunately comes for all of us.

The power that is in all of us is our sin nature. Occasionally we allow it to get out of control and when it does it can do considerable damage to our life and the lives of those close to us.

But, there is great news. God didn't leave us without hope to defeat the sin nature within us. He sent the Holy Spirit to fight within and alongside us to defeat that nature. Once we have the Holy Spirit, the Apostle Paul tells us that we, "however, are controlled not by the sinful nature but by the Spirit, if the Spirit of God lives in us."

Take control, allow God's Holy Spirit to drive out the sinful nature.

37

BLOOM WHERE YOU'RE PLANTED

2 Corinthians 2:14 (NASB)
But thanks be to God, who always leads us in triumph in Christ, and manifests through us the sweet aroma of the knowledge of Him in every place.

M y dad loved his garden and his fruit trees. He could have a very hard day and go out and weed his vegetables or prune his trees and the stress seemed to lift off him. I remember him teaching me about transplanting trees and plants and that you never did it when they were active as it could kill them or at the very least stunt them.

Unless we are running from Him, God has us right where he wants us. If we know that and allow Him to feed us, we will flourish right where we are. To decide we want to move, physically or emotionally somewhere else, we stand the chance of stunting our growth. God has us here for a reason and if He decides to move us, to uproot us and transplant us, it needs to be in His timing, not ours.

I remember an old saying, "Bloom where you're planted," it's so true with God. He has put us here today and wants us to bloom and thrive right where we are. If we fight Him we will shrivel and be of no use. Keep growing where He has you.

BLOOM WHERE YOU'RE PLANTED

_____

_____

_____

_____

_____

_____

_____

_____

NOTHING BUT THE BLOOD OF JESUS!

Hebrews 9:22
In fact, the law requires that nearly everything be cleansed with blood, and without the shedding of blood there is no forgiveness.

Blood is an amazing thing... In the physical and spiritual world both, the "lack" of blood means death. In the spiritual world the "loss" of blood means life.

I've written before that I love to blood trail animals. For a hunter, the bigger the trail, the more exciting the "track." Christ's blood is just the opposite... Only by the loss of His blood do we have hope for life, eternal life. More than anything else in the body, blood is essential to life. It's what carries the fuel and oxygen to the billions of cells in our bodies. Blood supplies the brain and the heart with the necessary nourishment to function. It also carries waste materials to the digestive system, where they are then removed from the body. Without blood we couldn't keep warm or cool, fight infections, or get rid of our own waste products. Additionally, our very identity—our DNA—is located in our blood.

Blood is what gives life, period! Both physical and spiritual life is dependent on Blood.

"For the life of the flesh is in the blood" Leviticus 17:11

If you are counting on ANYTHING else to get you through life, both now and the afterlife, you are going to be shocked by what you find...

NOTHING but the blood of Jesus!

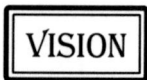

VISION

Jeremiah 29:11 (NIV)
"For I know the plans I have for you," declares the Lord, "plans to prosper you and not to harm you, plans to give you hope and a future."

As a guide we hold the very lives of hunters in our hands at times. Afternoons in the mountains can be unpredictable and a leisurely walk can suddenly turn into a fight for survival. Without a plan for the event of disaster we can get into trouble in a hurry. We plan to protect those that are in our care when things go bad.

In life we don't need to worry about whether or not there is a greater plan, God has it covered. We can trust God has a plan that will "prosper" us. This is not a promise of prospering financially; most of us have learned that there is so much more to prospering than getting rich.

God sees the end as well as the beginning, so He already knows what it will mean for us to "prosper." He has the vision to know what is best for us. He calls us to have vision as well, to look for what He has in store for us and step out in confidence, knowing that He has the net waiting below us, in case we fall.

Helen Keller was quoted, "Is there anything worse than being blind? Yes! The most pathetic person in the whole world is someone who has sight but has no vision."

Look beyond today, look beyond tomorrow, have the vision and confidence to live out what God has planned... Begin to prosper in Christ.

_____

_____

_____

_____

_____

_____

THE CALL OF TEMPTATION

Proverbs 6:20-24
My son, keep your father's command and do not forsake your mother's teaching. 21 Bind them always on your heart; fasten them around your neck. 22 When you walk, they will guide you; when you sleep, they will watch over you; when you awake, they will speak to you. 23 For this command is a lamp, this teaching is a light, and correction and instruction are the way to life, 24 keeping you from your neighbor's wife, from the smooth talk of a wayward woman.

This fall I had the amazing opportunity to experience almost the entire elk rut on the Cielo Vista Ranch in Southern Colorado. We guided from the last of August through yesterday. The bulls bugled the entire month but the last week it was deafening with the screams, groans and bellows of mature bulls. The cow elk calls we used were very effective for calling in the bulls. There were times when the bulls were coming from several directions. Four of the big bulls we killed were taken when bulls lost their sense of normal caution and succumbed to the urge to breed.... Coming to the "smooth talk" that they thought was a cow elk, causing their demise.

How often this happens to people... We desire something so much it doesn't matter what the danger is, we are going to do whatever it takes to get it.

King David is a prime example of this very thing. He saw a beautiful woman bathing and allowed his desire for her to override his morality. To David, his actions on that fateful night seemed trivial, just a momentary pause in an otherwise steadfast life. The consequences, however, were devastating, not just for David, or for Uriah, but also for David's family and the entire nation. The whole nation paid a high price for David's immorality.

In 2 Samuel 12:14, the prophet Nathan passes the bad news on to David of what will happen because he has given in to the "call of sin." Verse 14 "But because by doing this you have shown utter contempt for the Lord, the son born to you will die."

Like the elk that runs to the call, we will pay a price if we give in to temptation. We must focus on our relationship with God and run from the call of temptation. Proverbs 14:12 tells us, "There is a way that seems right to a man, but its end is the way of death."

ARE YOU LISTENING?

Deuteronomy 28:2
And all these blessings shall come upon you and overtake you
if you heed the voice of the Lord your God.

Tonight I was sitting high on a ridge waiting for dark to pick up my brother coming off the mountain. Being without a radio to hear when he was down I was spending the time glassing some elk. When all of a sudden from the valley below, I hear a voice yell out "Hey Dean!" I jumped up and yelled back, "What?" No response. I whistled… no response. So I drove the Ranger to the valley floor to find no one waiting. There was no one for 5 miles around.

I have no idea what I heard tonight on that quite mountain… It evidently wasn't human. Can God speak to us in an audible voice? He can do anything. I don't think that God called to me tonight, if He did, I'm not sure yet what He wanted.

But God does speak to us all the time. He speaks to us through His word, through other people that care enough about us to point out things in our lives, through His creation and many other ways.

Our job is to listen to His voice and respond.

In 1Samuel chapter 3 we read of Samuel hearing God call to him… Samuel's response was what our response needs to be… Verse 10, Then Samuel said, "Speak, for your servant is listening."

Are we, "His servants" listening as Samuel did?

Everything that happens in our lives, great or small, is a parable in which God speaks to us and the true grasping of these messages is to honestly hear God.

Are you listening?

WALLOWING

2 Corinthians 5:17
Therefore if anyone is in Christ, he is a new creature; the old things passed away; behold, new things have come.

Today we were cutting wood in a valley that's called wallow hollow. It's a place where the elk come down in the fall and the bulls roll around in the small puddles and cover themselves in mud. I've seen bulls, normally yellow in color, and come out of a wallow jet black. There is no way to go into a wallow and come out clean. Also bull elk wallow to cool down when they get over heated. People also go into a wallowing mood when they get over heated by something. When they don't get their way and get upset they often shut down in self pity and wallow for a time.

So, why do we "wallow" in our past? Why do we continue to sin when we are, "a new creation" as Paul put it?

We don't need to continue in our old lifestyle... We can be free of the chains that have held us.

1 John 1:9 tells us that, "If we confess our sins, He is faithful and righteous to forgive us our sins and to cleanse us from all unrighteousness."

The mud from the wallowing is washed clean... We are that "new creation."

So stop wallowing in your sins. God made you Holy so that you can be holy...

_____

_____

_____

_____

_____

_____

_____

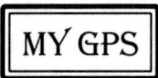

MY GPS

Psalm 32:8
"I will guide you and teach you the way you should go. I will give you good advice and watch over you."

G PS units have always fascinated me and I've owned three of them, but none have made it past the front door of the house. While I don't use mine, others have used their GPS to keep me from sleeping on the mountain.

One morning we watched a bunch of big bull elk above tree line and made a plan to get to them for the afternoon hunt. Well, afternoon turned into evening and evening turned into night. The hunting was so good we ended up a couple of long hard miles above and beyond the truck. Luckily Joe had his GPS in his pack with the truck marked.

The best GPS that I have is imbedded in my heart; it's my "God Positioning System". In life when we start to stray too far from where we should be or we head into trouble, this GPS will warn us. There is always a signal and the battery never needs replacing. We just have to trust it and never doubt it will show you the best path or the safest place.

Because I don't totally understand how my three GPS units work I have an issue with totally trusting them. However, with God, we can always trust His "God Positioning System."

Jerry Bridges wrote...
"God's plan and His ways of working out His plan are frequently beyond our ability to fathom and understand. We must learn to trust when we don't understand."

AIM SMALL, MISS SMALL

Philippians 3:12-14

12 Not that I have already obtained all this, or have already arrived at my goal, but I press on to take hold of that for which Christ Jesus took hold of me. 13 Brothers and sisters, I do not consider myself yet to have taken hold of it. But one thing I do: Forgetting what is behind and straining toward what is ahead, 14 I press on toward the goal to win the prize for which God has called me heavenward in Christ Jesus.

I love to shoot traditional archery gear. It is truly an art form. I can walk through the woods and pick out a leaf or a twig on the ground at 30 yards and hit it most every time. Now put a full grown deer at that same distance and I will miss it most of the time... Why, because I'm shooting at the entire deer, not at some as small as a twig.

I have a good friend that is a very good shot with his archery equipment. He can set up a target anywhere from 15 to 75 yards and keep his arrows in the center. He is always using the phrase, "aim small, miss small" and it works for him. This saying means that if we don't focus on the small important target we will miss our mark.

This same concept is true in life, if we don't concentrate on what is important we will go off in every direction, not doing what we should be doing.

Deuteronomy 7:6 says that we are a holy people. No one can be holy on their own, but if we "aim small" and strive towards holiness, we become better and better all the time. Verse 6...

"For you are a holy people to the LORD your God; the LORD your God has chosen you to be a people for His own possession out of all the peoples who are on the face of the earth."

Again, we can never attain holiness without a trust in Christ as our Savior. But once we have that relationship, we are then holy in God's eyes... But we will still struggle in our own hearts and lives.

So strive to be holy... Like in archery, the more you practice the better you will be.

"AIM SMALL, MISS SMALL"

EMPTY YOURSELF

Acts 4:31
And when they had prayed, the place where they had gathered together was shaken, and they were all filled with the Holy Spirit and began to speak the word of God with boldness.

T here is something special about a crisp fall morning. When you get into the woods for the first cold calm fall morning and take a deep breath, the moist cool air completely fills your lungs and actually feels like it fills your whole being. It's a refreshing, fulfilling experience that is hard to explain to someone that has never done it. There aren't many feelings like that... except to be filled with the Spirit of God.

The words, "to be filled with the Holy Spirit" have been explained differently by different people. But there is one thing that doesn't change... Like filling your lungs with crisp cold air takes emptying your body of the old air, to be filled with the Holy Spirit you need to completely empty yourself of you. There's no room for our own desires, needs or wants, just God's Spirit.

We've often heard that someone feels empty... We are never empty, we cannot be empty. We are either filled with God's wonderful spirit or we are filled with selfish desires.

Empty yourself of what you desire and allow God to fill you with His sweet spirit.

LIKE AN ARROW IN FLIGHT

Proverbs 13:20
Whoever walks with the wise becomes wise, but the companion
of fools will suffer harm.

I've loved archery since I was very little. My parents bought me a bright yellow fiberglass bow when I was about 8 years old and I loved shooting that bow. A few years ago a good friend made a beautiful little bow for Micah (our grandson). On the bow he wrote something like this, "May you never lose the joy of an arrow in flight."

What is it that keeps an arrow flying true? What makes it to fly straight toward its target and stabilizes it in flight? It is the fletching. Generally there are three of them.

And like the fletching of an arrow, we have things that stabilize us through life. I call them the three "S's". Allow these three S's to stabilize you through life. By dropping any one of them we lose stability. They are; the Scripture, the Saints and the Spirit.

The Scriptures in front of us, daily reading of God's word gives us direction. 1 Timothy 4:13 says, "Until I come, devote yourself to the public reading of Scripture, to exhortation, to teaching."

The Saints around us, surrounding ourselves with others that love the Lord will keep us "flying" a straight path. Proverbs 13:20

The Spirit inside us, once we've come to a saving relationship with Christ, the Holy Spirit indwells us and directs us by allowing us to see where we are going and speaks to us of right and wrong. 1 Timothy 4:13 tells us, "Until I come, devote yourself to the public reading of Scripture, to exhortation, to teaching."

Keep these three fletching, attached to your life at all times and you will fly straight. Try flying without them and you will drift off target... The longer you drift the harder it is to come back.

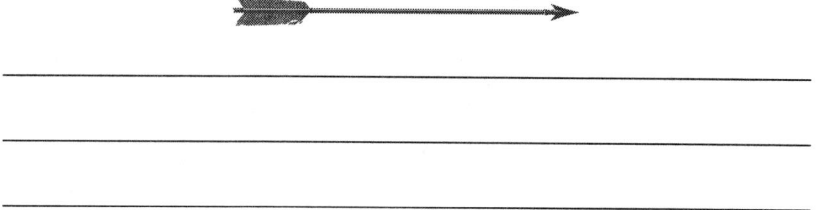

_____

_____

_____

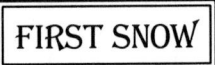

FIRST SNOW

2 Corinthians 5:17
Therefore if any man be in Christ, he is a new creature: old things are passed away; behold, all things are become new.

"There's fresh snow this morning," I said to Linda, as I glanced out the window into the predawn gray day. Linda moaned and rolled over. I guess growing up in the UP of Michigan you might assume that we would be a cold weather, winter type people. In reality, winter is something I have never looked forward to.

It seems like all the life and energy of the summer dwindles away as birds fly south, and insects disappear. The days become shorter, and even the bright sun doesn't seem as bright or as warm. Instead, with every second you stay outside you grow colder and colder.

Yet today, something else crossed my mind. There really isn't anything like the first snowfall, which leaves the ground a fluffy pure white, free from any dirt or debris. Immediately, my mood shifted from one of coldness and bitterness, to one of awe for what God can do with any situation.

While the winter may not be as warm as the summer, or have the same characteristics, God makes it special and wonderful in its own way. The same way He does with all of us. But regardless, God makes all things anew, clean and beautiful in His (and our) site. In Romans 8:28 we see that He takes our past situation, and makes it work out for His glory.

Today, remember how God has changed and improved your life. Remember the power that He holds, power to take any situation and make it good. And when you see someone who needs God, think just that... and then share His love story with them.

Godly change (like the season) is always good.

STRADDLING THE FENCE

Romans 1:16
For I am not ashamed of the gospel of Christ: for it is the power of God unto salvation to everyone that believeth; to the Jew first, and also to the Greek.

Yesterday Linda and I were riding in the car and on the radio we heard that someone was "straddling the fence" on an issue. Linda said, "That sounds painful." I chuckled and agreed... I've accidentally straddled wooden fences, barbed wire fences and even one electric fence... They were all painful.

I'm getting too old to straddle fences, both literally and figuratively. We have to come to a point in our lives where we take a stand and live through it. If you are a Christian you have to eventually say, "I'm not ashamed of the gospel of Christ" and stick to it. If you don't you are wasting the greatest gift that God can give, the Gift of His one and only Son (John 3:16)

There is an Aaron Tippin song named YOU"VE GOT TO FOLLOW SOMETHING. If we read into this song as the "family" being the Family of God, it speaks right to our need to stand up for what Christ has done for us.

You've got to stand for something or you'll fall for anything
You've got to be your own man not a puppet on a string
Never compromise what's right and uphold your family name
You've got to stand for something or you'll fall for anything

We are coming into a time where we will be called out to stand for something... Where will you stand?

Matthew 5:10
Blessed are those who are persecuted for righteousness' sake, for theirs is the kingdom of heaven.

49

NEW GROWTH

Ephesians 4:22-24 (ESV)
[22] to put off your old self, which belongs to your former manner of life and is corrupt through deceitful desires, [23] and to be renewed in the spirit of your minds, [24] and to put on the new self, created after the likeness of God in true righteousness and holiness.

Yesterday I pulled some trail camera cards over some mineral sites. This time of the year isn't nearly as exciting as fall, but it is always fun to see what is happening with the deer. What I saw was good news. There were several bucks that were showing some early growth; a couple of them were mature deer that made it through last season and through our Upper Peninsula winter.

Each year the males of the deer species drop the old dead "bone" from their head and replace it with new growth. In a healthy deer the new growth is bigger and stronger than the antler that was discarded earlier.

Life in Christ is designed to be like the new growth of deer antlers. God gives us new life, Christ came to shed off the old and build up the new. The law of the Old Testament was replaced with freedom of the New Testament. Unfortunately, many Christians do not ever live out the freedoms that Christ gives us. They live as though they still are carrying around the old growth and the new growth can't get a foothold. They fear what might happen if they step out in life and allow Christ to work through them, they stay in a state of dormancy.

1 John 4:18 tells us that with Christ there is no fear.

There is no fear in love, but perfect love casts out fear. For fear has to do with punishment, and whoever fears has not been perfected in love.

Accept the gift of the new life in Christ. Many have accepted the gift of a salvation but have never put in motion the new life.

Shed the old, allow the new to grow.

_____

_____

_____

TROPHIES OF GRACE

2 Corinthians 2:14

"But thanks be to God! For through what Christ has done, He has triumphed over us so that now wherever we go He uses us to tell others about the Lord and to spread the Gospel like a sweet perfume."

L inda and I along with our sons (mostly Linda) have put together a fairly good number of trophy mounts in our home and camp. These are similar to a football, tennis or basketball player's showcase where he or she would display their awards. Each of the "trophies" on display carries a special memory or triumph in life.

If today you know Christ as your personal Savior, you are a trophy of His grace.

One definition of God's grace is this, "the free and unmerited favor of God, as manifested in the salvation of sinners and the bestowal of blessings."

So as Christians we can think of ourselves as God's trophies on display in heaven for eternity. Because of His grace we are justified, purified and His forever more. We were purchased with the very blood of God's only Son (John 3:16).

Joseph Price said, "If it is God who justifies you, who can bring a charge against you?"

So if we are TROPHIES OF GOD'S GRACE, who can stand against the power of an almighty God. Stand firm.

———————————————————————

———————————————————————

———————————————————————

———————————————————————

———————————————————————

———————————————————————

———————————————————————

LIKE A ROARING LION

1 Peter 5:8-9

"Be alert and of sober mind. Your enemy the devil prowls around like a roaring lion looking for someone to devour. Resist him, standing firm in the faith, because you know that the family of believers throughout the world is undergoing the same kind of sufferings."

One of my favorite, all-time movies is, <u>Ghosts in the Darkness</u>. I'm not sure why, because I am not usually one for blood and gore. The two stars of that movie are two huge male lions that I associate with these verses. These two lions roam at night, in the darkness, searching for some to devour.

These verses describe this very thing. But we are called to be sober. Not just sober physically, but spiritually... prepared to resist Satan at every turn. If we "sleep", or doze off in our spiritual life, Satan is waiting right there to overtake us.

So prepare yourself, stay spiritually awake, and don't convince yourself that you can't stray off of God's path just a little ways. Off His path is darkness and this darkness is where Satan lurks to take us down.

Instead, "Submit yourselves therefore to God, resist the devil, and he will flee from you." James 4:7

And finally there is a reward for remaining sober and resisting.

James 1:12 – "Blessed is the man that endures temptation: for when he is tried, he shall receive the crown of life, which the Lord hath promised to them that love him."

TRUE NORTH

Romans 8:28

"And we know that God causes all things to work together for good to those who love God, to those who are called according to His purpose." This verse doesn't promise that all things will be easy for those who love God. However, they promise that they will "work together for good."

Thee is a line in the movie LINCOLN where Abraham Lincoln says,

"A compass, I learnt when I was surveying, it'll... it'll point you True North from where you're standing, but it's got no advice about the swamps and dessert and chasm that you'll encounter along the way. If in pursuit of your destination, you plunge ahead, heedless of obstacles, and achieve nothing more than to sink in a swamp... What's the use of knowing True North?"

This is a great line that is true in human thinking. However, in a life where God is allowed to fill us and we are loving and trusting Him, we need not worry about the swamps, desserts and chasms of life. This is true in the outdoors as well. We can see the big dipper and the North Star, we can have a compass in our hand... we can follow them day and night ... but we will still come up against obstacles.

God will get us through them. And, if we trust Him to do so, we will be blessed each time we come out of one of them and HE will be glorified. This is only true if we are filled with a love for God and that we have that personal relationship with Him.

Allow God to direct your *"compass" in life and His "true north" will always be reachable, with Him as your guide.

_____

_____

_____

_____

_____

_____

PLANTING SEEDS

Matthew 25:35-40

"For I was hungry and you gave me food, I was thirsty and you gave me drink, I was a stranger and you welcomed me, I was naked and you clothed me, I was sick and you visited me, I was in prison and you came to me. Then the righteous will answer him, saying, Lord, when did we see you hungry and feed you, or thirsty and give you drink? And when did we see you a stranger and welcome you, or naked and clothe you? And when did we see you sick or in prison and visit you? And the King will answer them, Truly, I say to you, as you did it to one of the least of these my brothers, you did it to me."

Throughout our lives when, we serve others, we have no way of knowing how it effects their lives. As the verse above states, "Lord when did we see you hungry and feed you?"

This weekend I was told a story about a disabled veteran who was served by some others. He was treated to a very special hunt and at the end of the weekend he spoke from his wheelchair... "A short time back I loaded a pistol and held it to my head, when I pulled the trigger the round didn't fire." He pulled out a loaded round of ammo, held it up and continued. "Because of this hunt, I will ever need this again."

We are called to serve each other, to love each other and to look out for each other... We have no idea the eternal impact we have by our actions.

Our job is to "plant seeds" and "water" them... God does the rest. Like putting in a food plot for a fall hunt, if we don't first put the seeds in the ground there isn't much chance that it will produce a harvest come season.

1 Corinthians 3:7

"It's not important who does the planting, or who does the watering. What's important is that God makes the seed grow."

_____

_____

_____

_____

JUST ASK, HE WILL ANSWER

Matt 7:7
"Ask and it will be given to you, seek and you will find, knock and the door will be opened to you."

I t had been a long morning. Jim and I had hunted up a big ridge above Uyak Bay on Kodiak Island since daylight, now it was approaching noon. We had fought brush all the way. We were looking for a place to glass for blacktail deer. Finally finding no openings in the brush big enough, we decided to walk back down through a mile of narrow creek bottom.

Walking in these types of confined areas, in the middle of brown bear haunts was not the best idea, but it was easier than where we had been walking.

A few minutes into our decent we jumped a deer and it was soon swallowed up by the thick brush. Instinctively, I let out a call like a distressed fawn, in an attempt to call it back. Instead of a deer coming to the call, a huge, half ton, charging bear came crashing in looking for an easy meal. Luckily for me, Jim panicked and pulled the trigger on his rifle stopping the bear at about 20 ft. As the bear turned to leave I started praying for God's protection for Jim and myself. We escaped out of the creek bottom to the ridge above. We were in a bad spot and needed to get out quickly; God provided the way and saved our lives that day.

Too many people are not persistent in their asking, seeking and knocking so they are unable to find the way out of their problems. God promises to provide a way out of our problems. It is sure but it is conditioned upon our determination to ask, seek and knock until He opens the best door.

Remember the way we think is the best isn't always so. Sometimes we think the valley is the place to get out, when it was really the ridge top. To find the way, we have to ask.

Isa. 55:8-9
"For my thoughts are not your thoughts, neither are your ways my ways, declares the Lord. As the heavens are higher than the earth, so are my ways higher your ways and my thoughts than your thoughts."

APPLE SEEDS

John 4:35-38

"Do you not say, 'There are yet four months, and then comes the harvest'?
Behold, I say to you, lift up your eyes and look on the fields, that they are
white for harvest. "Already he who reaps is receiving wages and is gathering
fruit for life eternal; so that he who sows and he who reaps may rejoice
together "For in this case the saying is true, 'One sows and another reaps.'
"I sent you to reap that for which you have not labored; others have labored
and you have entered into their labor."

We are called to sow seeds concerning Christ and what He did for us,
His love and the hope we have through Him. We are called to sow in
faith, faith that there will be a harvest and it might not be us involved in the
harvest... But we do our part.

There are four principals of sowing and reaping:

- You reap what you sow. If you sow apple seeds, you get apples,
  not sugar cane.
- You can only reap if you sow. If you don't sow the seeds, how
  will it grow?
- The harvest takes time. Wait on the harvest. Tend to the crop. In due
  season we shall reap (if we faint not).
- You will reap more than what you sow.

My uncle planted an Oak tree in his yard about 20 years ago with an acorn
he picked up at a local park. Every year that tree yields thousands of acorns.
Consider the apple tree; planted with one seed. Think of how many apples
that tree produces just in one season. Then think how many seeds are in
those apples. Now think of this; any man can count the number of seeds in
an apple, but only God can count the number of apples in a seed! Praise the
Lord for His magnificence!"

What a great thought... We can plant one seed about Christ. That one seed
can multiply into millions in heaven. Our job is just to sow seeds.

Remember the APPLE SEEDS.

STRAP IN!

Psalm 27:1
"The Lord is my light and my salvation, whom shall I fear?
The Lord is the stronghold of my life, of whom shall I be afraid?"

When you've guided hunters for a few slow days of hunting you get to know a lot about them. You're always looking for something to break up the monotony of the long days. This was the case with Bill... Bill was a hunter from northern Illinois who walked with a pronounced limp. After a of couple days of slow elk hunting somehow conversation turned to his limp.

Bill told me a horrific story of falling from a tree stand on to a metal fence post. He explained in depth the terrible details of being impaled, the surgeries and then the long years of recovery; all because he didn't wear a safety harness, a very simple insurance against pain or death.

It made me realize that Christ can be a safety harness of sorts. He insures us a life without ultimate death (eternal life). But in this life Christ also, like a tree stand harness, allows us a freedom to move about without fear.

While a harness attaches us to the tree and would seem to limit us, it actually is giving us freedom without fear. We know that if we make a misstep we are not in danger of disaster. Yes, we may feel a little pain if we fall, but our safety harness will hold us and allows us an assurance that we are safe.

Going through life without a relationship with Christ is like leaning out over the edge of a tree stand. You might be OK for today, but eventually you will pay the ultimate consequence.

Be safe and strap into the eternal safety harness. If you don't have this safety harness in your life, please feel free to contact me with any questions. If you already have the connection with Christ, share it with those around you. You wouldn't watch your friends lean out of a tree stand without mentioning a safety harness... Don't let them live without knowing Christ, the ultimate "Safety Harness."

Strap in.

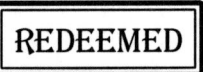

REDEEMED

Titus 2:14
"Who gave Himself for us to redeem us from every lawless deed, and to purify for Himself a people for His own possession, zealous for good deeds."

A few years ago while on a deer hunt, I spent a morning with a good friend, Brandt. That morning will live on in our memories forever, funny to mine, sad to Brandt's.

That morning a huge 150" 9 point buck chased a doe right out in front of us. Brandt proceeded to fire several shots at the buck, but each and every shot missed its mark. Brandt's head just hung at his chest... The best I could do was to tell him, "This won't make any difference in your life tomorrow." After a couple hours at the rifle range, Linda took Brandt out for the afternoon hunt. About sunset I got a call asking me to come pick the two of them up as they had shot at a buck. When I arrived Brandt was standing over a great 13 point buck... Bigger than the morning's buck. Brandt had redeemed himself. But we still laugh at the morning's fiasco.

I can't speak for anyone else but I know that like Brandt did with the deer, I miss the mark in life on a daily basis. Romans 3:23 tells us that, "All have sinned and fallen short of the glory of God." We all need to be redeemed. The important thing is to know that my redemption has been taken care of once and for all by what Christ did for me 2,000 years ago (John 3:16). I don't have to go back and redeem myself.

So next time you miss the mark in life, know that Christ paid the price for that. If you've accepted His gift to you then you are already redeemed... If you haven't accepted that gift, know that your redemption has already been paid... You just have to accept it.

Big Daddy Weave recorded a song called "Redeemed." The first verse says it well...
I am redeemed, You set me free
So I'll shake off these heavy chains
Wipe away every stain, now I'm not who I used to be
I am redeemed, I'm redeemed"... REDEEMED

STAND THE TEST

James 1:12
"Blessed is the one who perseveres under trial because, having stood the test, that person will receive the crown of life that the Lord has promised to those who love him."

Our lives are filled with trials... Today mine was filled with high winds and driving rain... Along with very unseasonably warm temperatures. When guiding for deer this combination can be, and this week is, a recipe for disaster. But I keep telling myself that I can't do much of anything about nature... It's taken me years to realize I can only control the things that God has put under my control. Once we realize that God has control of everything and allows only certain things to fall within our realm of influence only then do we allow ourselves to totally trust Him. We will have pain and trials. We will go through bad times... But we can trust Him 110%

Vince Lombardi once said...

"Once you agree upon the price you must pay for success, it enables you to ignore the minor hurts, the opponent's pressure, and the temporary failures."

Satan will attack God's people. We will face temporary pain and suffering. But we know, without a shadow of a doubt that God will carry us through.

Stand the test!

YOUR GUIDE

Psalm 23:1-4

1 The Lord is my shepherd, I lack nothing. 2 He makes me lie down in green pastures, He leads me beside quiet waters, 3 He refreshes my soul. He guides me along the right paths for his name's sake. 4 Even though I walk through the darkest valley, I will fear no evil, for you are with me; your rod and your staff, they comfort me.

I'm starting my 30th year of guiding this year. It doesn't seem possible until I look back on all of the great friends that I've made over that time. I do have some friends that always tell me they wouldn't go on a guided hunt as they would always prefer to do it all themselves.

There are some places hunting on your own is not legal and if you want to hunt there you are required to have a licensed guide with you. Why? It is to protect you from the dangers. For instance a non-resident hunter in Alaska is required by law to have a guide for grizzly bears, sheep etc... Without a guide your life is in danger in many situations on these trips.

This is the case with life in general. We have a need for a guide in our lives. Most everyone has heard and/or memorized the 23rd Psalm. These verses speak of a shepherd that is caring for His sheep.

Life is dangerous and we could also use a guide. He is always there and all too often we ignore His advice and guiding. When we do this we end up in terrible trouble. Stick close to your Guide in life.

When times are dark your Guide will light your way for you. He holds the light that illuminates our way in life.

Psalms 119:105, Thy word is a lamp unto my feet, and a light unto my path.

Use your guide regularly.

HAVE THE OLD THINGS PASSED AWAY?

2 Corinthians 5:17
Therefore if any man be in Christ, he is a new creature: old things are passed away; behold, all things have become new.

A caterpillar is an interesting insect in many ways. However, it would rarely be called beautiful. At some point in its life it creates this shell called a cocoon around itself. This cocoon isn't very pretty either. Sometime later it emerges from this shell a totally new and different creation. Now it is amazingly beautiful... AND IT FLIES!!

This a great symbol of lives that come to trust in Christ, "old things are passed away, all things are new". We no longer have to crawl through life struggling to get over obstacles on our own efforts, we are released to fly.

If the new creation, the beautiful butterfly, tried to carry the shell of the caterpillar around so it could live in its old life... It will never be able to fly. Once one comes to Christ, we are free from carrying the burdens of our past. Like the caterpillar turned butterfly we have lift under our wings in life. Christ is what lifts us.

Let go of your past... Learn to fly... You are a new creation.

_____

_____

_____

_____

_____

_____

_____

_____

_____

TIE IT ON YOUR HEART

Deuteronomy 11:18-19 (NIV)
Fix these words of mine in your hearts and minds; tie them as symbols on your hands and bind them on your foreheads. 19 Teach them to your children, talking about them when you sit at home and when you walk along the road, when you lie down and when you get up.

All of us that hunt have heard the stories of someone pulling their bow or rifle up into a tree stand and have the rope break or the knot come undone. I once watched my favorite rifle free fall 20' to the base of a large spruce tree. It is a sick feeling. I've got a friend that won't hunt one of my stands anymore because he saw his Mathews Bow clatter down the rungs of the tree stand.

Our hunting equipment is precious to many of us and we treat it like our babies at times. If only we were to treat our spiritual life with the same care and conviction all of the time. We passively live a "good life" and attend church on Sunday. We talk the talk on Sunday and maybe throughout the week... But do we walk the walk?

If we can just learn to cherish God's word like we do our "things" in this life. Verse 18 says to, "tie them as symbols on your hands and bind them on your foreheads." This is so we can never forget them or be without them.

Just as we are taught to do things as a child, we learn to do spiritual things by repetition and internalizing meanings... So it is with a close Christian walk. We need to continually surround ourselves with Godly people and Godly things.

Once when a skeptic expressed surprise to see him reading a Bible, Abraham Lincoln said, "Take all that you can of this book upon reason, and the balance on faith, and you will live and die a happier man."

Take all that is important and tie it on your heart.

THE TRUE CALL

John 6:44 (NIV)
No one can come to me unless the Father who sent me draws him.
And I will raise him up on the last day.

Turkey hunters are a devoted group... yet they are all a little off center. They are a group who will swear off sleep for weeks on end just to match wits with a bird with a brain the size of a small walnut, a group that will sit motionless for hours hoping to outsmart a stupid bird using calls and decoys.

When turkey hunting, most hunters utilize their calls of varying types as well as decoys to try to bring a gobbler into range. Some days it works and other days it doesn't. When it does work for the hunter, the turkey will be fooled by the call and the look of a "false" turkey... Coming close enough to be harvested and later eaten.

Then there are other hunts where the turkeys can discern that the calling isn't real and the decoy is just a substitute for the real thing.

Life is just like that, for every one of us. We will all be called to something. We will all make a decision in life to go to what is true and real or to go to a false calling. As in turkey hunting, going to a call that isn't true and from God can only lead to one thing, DEATH. This is an eternal death that damns us forever in the torment of hell.

Our other option is to go to the calling of the truth. In John 14 Jesus tells us who and what the truth is.

Verse 6 Jesus answered, "I am the way, the truth and the life. No one comes to the Father except through me."

While going to the false call brings eternal death and damnation, going to the true calling, that is Christ, gives you eternal life in heaven. Jesus is that truth, the life and the one and only way to heaven.

Don't be fooled by the false calls and pretty decoys of the world... Satan is an amazing hunter of men and women's souls...

1 Peter 5:8 (NIV) tells us
Be alert and of sober mind. Your enemy the devil prowls around like a roaring lion looking for someone to devour.

Respond to the true call.

BEING WATCHED

Titus 2:12 (NASB)
Instructing us to deny ungodliness and worldly desires and to live sensibly, righteously and Godly in the present age,

A few years ago on Kodiak Island Linda and I hunted black tail deer in an area that was covered with Brown Bear sign. There were tracks and droppings everywhere you looked. We had a feeling that we were being watched all the time. We got out safely, thank God, but it was a bad feeling that we were under the scrutiny of dangerous bears.

We need to realize that in our lives, we are always under the watchful eye of others. If we are going to claim to be something godly then we had better live up to that. People are watching and waiting for Christians to screw up and if and when we do, we will be pounced upon. It is similar to the grizzlies in Alaska, in the dark waiting for something to devour.

This doesn't mean that we let people walk on us or try to hide who we are... It means we speak the truth in love and do our best always to lead godly lives.

So what is the trick to staying in the right place?

Elizabeth George said, "When you cultivate a godly thought life your soul will shine and you will exhibit the presence of the Lord in you."

Ephesians 5:15-17(NASB)
Therefore be careful how you walk, not as unwise men but as wise, 16 making the most of your time, because the days are evil. 17 So then do not be foolish, but understand what the will of the Lord is.

SPIRITUAL "TRAINING"

Romans 8:16-18 (NIV)

The Spirit himself testifies with our spirit that we are God's children. 17 Now if we are children, then we are heirs—heirs of God and co-heirs with Christ, if indeed we share in his sufferings in order that we may also share in his glory. 18 I consider that our present sufferings are not worth comparing with the glory that will be revealed in us.

My friend Ryan has been in training for the last two years for hunting in the mountains. He pushes himself really hard every day. He climbs hundreds of stairs on Pine Mountain with a back pack, eats right and pushes himself to the limit. His reward is the glory of being in shape to reach places in the mountains that the rest of us can't reach and hopefully to get a trophy elk.

The Christian life is kind of like this; if we are truly living for Christ. We take beatings (mostly figuratively) and we strain to do what Christ would have us do. We strive to grow and get our hearts in shape and in line with His. All to one day receive the crowning glory that awaits us, to hear the words, "well done my good and faithful servant."

John 16:33(KJV) tells us that we will pay a price... "These things I have spoken unto you, that in me you might have peace. In the world you shall have tribulation: but be of good cheer; I have overcome the world."

So if you are not, "sharing in His suffering" and not "having tribulations," start to examine your heart. In order to receive His glory we are told we must go through these things.

Ryan will probably see the glory of the back country and probably take another elk this year... Why, because he went through the sufferings. How about you? Will you get to experience the glory promised? Are you training to get to His glory?

_____

_____

_____

_____

WAIT ON HIM

1 Samuel 13:13-14 (NIV)

"You have done a foolish thing," Samuel said. "You have not kept the command the Lord your God gave you; if you had, he would have established your kingdom over Israel for all time. 14 But now your kingdom will not endure; the Lord has sought out a man after his own heart and appointed him ruler of his people, because you have not kept the Lord's command."

C alling turkeys is a passion of mine. I love to get turkeys as well as elk, deer, owls even songbirds like cardinals and chickadees to come to me. When hunting elk and turkeys, calling is a huge part of the game, but patience is even bigger. Knowing the right time to move, to stalk, to call more or just to sit silently, these are the times of patience and discerning.

Our life is like this. We have goals and plans and God has given us promises and direction. Moving ahead of God will always cause hardship and disappointment. Consider Abraham, God promised him a son and Abraham and Sarah didn't wait on the Lord... They thought they knew better and the world is paying for their lack of patience and disobedience yet today.

Two of the hardest tests on the spiritual road are the patience to wait for the right moment and the courage to move forward when the right time comes.

Saul didn't wait as he was told and his family line was cut off as the kings of Israel. Now we might not pay that price but if we don't wait on the Lord, it will have huge effects.

Listen to God's word, look for the promises and most importantly, wait on Him.

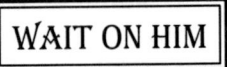

_____

_____

_____

_____

_____

_____

DON'T WORRY... BUT PLAN

Matthew 6:33-34 (NIV)
But seek first his kingdom and his righteousness, and all these things will
be given to you as well. 34 Therefore do not worry about tomorrow, for
tomorrow will worry about itself. Each day has enough trouble of its own.

I love planning for a hunting trip... It is almost as much fun as the trip itself. I lay maps out on the table and study. I pack, unpack, repack and then add more. I meet with my travel companions to plan and plot a course. It is so exciting for me. A trip without a good plan can turn into a disaster in a hurry. Who's bringing the food, and the drinks, what will I bring for clothes to cover whatever the weather condition?

In life we often fail to look ahead. In Matthew it says not to worry about tomorrow, it doesn't say that we shouldn't plan for tomorrow. In our country, the chances of dying of thirst or hunger or going naked are slim... But if we don't plan we may run into some rough times in life.

God gives us a brain to think ahead. He gives us friends with wisdom to help direct us... We need to use that which God has given us.

Proverbs 15:22(NIV) explains it well.
"Plans fail for lack of counsel, but with many advisers they succeed."

Don't worry... But plan!

_____

_____

_____

_____

_____

_____

_____

PRESCRIBED BURN

1 Peter 4:12-13 (ESV)
Beloved, do not be surprised at the fiery trial when it comes upon you to test you, as though something strange were happening to you. 13 But rejoice insofar as you share Christ's sufferings that you may also rejoice and be glad when his glory is revealed.

Wildlife habitat can become overgrown and the food that was once there is no longer useful. It is tough and the nutrition that was once abundant is now gone. As the plant life became tough it was of no use.

The same can be true of people. When we are young in our Christian walk we grow quickly and we are useful to Christ and to others. Some of us become toughened and bitter and the spiritual "nutrition" that we once shared goes away.

A habitat biologist will use prescribed burns that will bring back new growth to the plant life there. Peter writes that we shouldn't be surprised when "fiery trials comes upon us." Like the plants, these fiery trials produce new, tender growth in our lives, tender growth that is usable and is "nutritious" to us and to those around us.

So welcome trials as they come, stand firm in your faith. Look toward the coming glory that will be revealed.

STRENGTH IN NUMBERS

Ecclesiastes 4:9–12 (ESV)
Two are better than one, because they have a good reward for their toil. 10 For if they fall, one will lift up his fellow. But woe to him who is alone when he falls and has not another to lift him up! 11 Again, if two lie together, they keep warm, but how can one keep warm alone? 12 And though a man might prevail against one who is alone, two will withstand him— a threefold cord is not quickly broken.

I have always enjoyed archery. As a kid at bible camp I won trophies most years. I still love the curves and contours of a recurve bow. As children, most of us have bent a piece of wood and tied a string on and we were able to shoot an arrow a short way. But soon that bow breaks. A good bow builder will attach layers of lamination to support each other and strength the bow. So it is with people, if we surround ourselves with other like minded people we can stand up to so much more.

It's like a red hot ember in a fire. It will stay red and extremely hot if it remains in with the rest of the coals. But pull it out on its own and it soon turns cold and gray.

Hebrews 10:24–25
And let us consider how to stir up one another to love and good works, 25 not neglecting to meet together, as is the habit of some, but encouraging one another, and all the more as you see the Day drawing near.

So surround yourself with strong Christians. Hold each other up.

_____

_____

_____

_____

_____

_____

_____

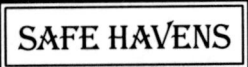

SAFE HAVENS

James 5:16 (NIV)
"Therefore confess your sins to each other and pray for each other so that you may be healed. The prayer of a righteous person is powerful and effective."

An elk herd will usually climb to a high mountain bench before lying down for the day. They will get to a safe place, generally with several other elk. While some sleep, others are alert and watching for danger. They work as a team protecting one another. So it should be with people.

In the first sentence of this verse, Christians are directed to confess their faults one to another, and so to join in their prayers with and for one another. It also indicates that there are some illnesses that are caused by our sins. Not all illness is a result of sin, but certainly some are.

So we are directed to have those around us who we can safely confess our sins and struggles. Everyone needs someone that they can rely on to hold them up and hold them accountable. We need a safe place and a godly person to pray for us.

Then a great promise, "The prayer of a righteous person is powerful and effective." Like the elk, there is power in those around you who are always looking out for you.

Find that person that loves you enough to pray for you and allows you a safe haven. And go be that person for someone else.

A HARD ROAD

Matthew 7:14 (ESV)
"For the gate is narrow and the way is hard that leads to life,
and those who find it are few."

I love the mountains, but my body and lungs hate climbing the mountains ...however, you can't really appreciate the mountains without climbing. You look ahead at the hard road and keep trudging forward and it is tough. When you get to the summit you turn and look back to see where you've been; it's generally very beautiful.

This is the life of one who knows the Lord. We've been promised that life will be hard, but the results are not only worth it, they are eternal.

So if you've chosen the narrow gate, keep "fighting the good fight"... in the future when you look back, you will see the blessings were well worth the struggle. If you don't know Christ and you are taking the easy road, consider the future and your eternity. Remember this, nothing worthwhile is ever easy.

Matthew 7:13-14 (ESV)
" Enter by the narrow gate. For the gate is wide and the way is easy that leads to destruction, and those who enter by it are many. 14 For the gate is narrow and the way is hard that leads to life, and those who find it are few."

_____

_____

_____

_____

_____

_____

_____

_____

_____

71

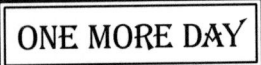

ONE MORE DAY

Isaiah 53:5 (KJV)
"But He was wounded for our transgressions, He was bruised for our iniquities; the chastisement for our peace was upon Him, and by His stripes we are healed."

The day started out innocent enough; the guys at camp decided to take a mule and horse ride into North Vallejos Basin and seeing it was my birthday, I was their special guest. It didn't seem to matter to any of them that I had not been on a horse for 10+ years and the ride might be a long one but more importantly, we didn't know if there was any kind of trail to follow.

Well, my lack of riding was not a problem for the first couple hours but the lack of trail and the distance caused major pain by the end of the day. As we rode I wondered why the others wore their sleeves down on such a warm day, I was soon to find out.

We busted through spruce timber and climbed over rock slides, across rushing streams and through aspen stands whose beauty couldn't be captured by a camera or paint brush. By the end of the day we had ridden 20 long, rough miles and when we arrived back at camp I had to be helped off the horse and into my bedroom where I promptly fell on the bed.

I suffered tremendous pain in my lower back and hips as well as my arms where it looked as though someone had taken a whip to me. As I looked at my arms and the blood that was flowing from the cuts I imagined what Christ had gone through in His last days on earth. My pain and suffering couldn't come close to comparing to what He did…and did for me. He was wounded for MY transgressions and He was bruised for MY iniquities. What a gift.

Christ doesn't expect us to repay Him for what He did on the cross, He just asks us to accept His gift of His death and resurrection offer.

Have you accepted this greatest gift from Christ? Have you thanked Him for what He went through for you? If not, do both today, don't put it off one more day.

Thank you Lord for what you have done for me, Amen!

A BETTER PLAN

Genesis 50:20 (NIV)
You intended to harm me, but God intended it for good to accomplish what is now being done, the saving of many lives.

In the book of Job, we read that Job could have very easily cursed God and died when he lost everything. In Genesis, Joseph could have felt sorry for himself or had his brothers put to death or imprisoned. Paul could have called on God to change his circumstances many times... But they all trusted God and knew that He had a plan for their lives.

On one evening's elk hunt we were above timber line and two to three rough miles from the truck. We were calling to a good bull elk for a friend. The excitement had built over a 45 minute calling sequence where the bull bugled continually. Finally the bull stepped out above the trees into the open. There were only a few stunted Alpine spruce scattered about.

When the bull finally turned broadside I was looking right over the hunters shoulder and right down his arrow. On release I watched the arrow's flight. All looked good, but then a small branch was just an inch too long and the arrow sailed off over the bull's back and off the edge of the mountain. Turning to my brother Dave, who had been calling from behind me, he smiled and point way off in the distance toward the truck, then he said, "I've never been so happy to see an arrow fly over a bulls back."

We thought we had that bull, and we should have except for one small twig. We also thought we wanted the bull, and later found that we would have suffered badly in getting him off the mountain. What we wanted wasn't what was best.

Sometimes God doesn't give us what we think we want. Sometimes it's because He has a better plan right away and sometimes it's because He is protecting us from something worse in the future. Rest assured He has a plan and we will be blessed because of it, if we trust Him.

A LIGHT TO THE WORLD

John 8:12 (NIV)
When Jesus spoke again to the people, he said, "I am the light of the world. Whoever follows me will never walk in darkness, but will have the light of life."

I enjoy walking into the woods in the morning darkness... Not total darkness, but when there is just enough light to make out where I am going. Last year I tried to walk out on a high Colorado ridge in total darkness, I made it about 20 yards and dug out my flashlight. I was in a really dangerous situation without a light to shine my way.

In life, Christ is that light. He opens our eyes to the dangers around us and... If we allow Him, he illuminates the correct path. Once we have that true relationship with Christ, we then become light. We shine to show the world the difference between good and bad.

If you are not that light, take some time to consider where your heart is at this point in your life. The Bible doesn't say we "might" be or "can" be... It says if we know Him, we "are" the light. Be the light.

_____

_____

_____

_____

_____

_____

_____

_____

_____

FORGETTING YOUR PAST

Philippians 3:13-14 (NIV)
Brothers and sisters, I do not consider myself yet to have taken hold of it. But one thing I do: Forgetting what is behind and straining toward what is ahead, 14 I press on toward the goal to win the prize for which God has called me heavenward in Christ Jesus.

It is sad to think how often we allow ourselves to live in the past. We spent countless, wasted, hours thinking of the bad decisions and actions that we've made. This only takes away from what we can do in our future.

For those that are hunters, if we allow past mistakes and choices to drag us down we never become a better hunter. Drawing our bow at the wrong time, setting up with the wrong wind, calling at the wrong time or moving when game is in sight can all spoil an otherwise successful hunt. We can't live in the past allowing these things to control our actions, however, we learn from those things to make our future more successful... The same is true with the rest of life.

The apostle Paul spent his young adult life killing the followers of Christ. Yet later in life, once he himself became a follower, he tells us, "forgetting what is behind and straining toward what is ahead"... He was free from his past.

This freedom can only come from Christ. Without Him we are bound to our past, with Him, our past is totally forgiven.

Move forward, leave your past behind, don't worry about what others think and "press on toward the goal to win the prize for which God has called me heavenward in Christ."

IMITATION

Ephesians 5:1-2 (NIV)
Follow God's example, therefore, as dearly loved children and walk in the way of love, just as Christ loved us and gave Himself up for us as a fragrant offering and sacrifice to God.

In my basement and garage you will find several different kinds of decoys: duck, goose, deer, turkey and elk etc... I have more game calls than I could use in three lifetimes, bugles, box calls, tube calls, slate calls, diaphragm calls, grunt calls, owl calls etc...

I rarely go in the woods without imitating something; it's one of my favorite parts of hunting.

In our lives as Christians, we have but One to imitate, Jesus Christ. One of the ways Jesus taught us to imitate God is by loving those He came to seek and to save. He loved us, even to the point of death. That is being like God; and that is what is going to attract others and accept His gift of salvation.

John 13:35 (NIV) says, "By this everyone will know that you are my disciples, if you love one another."

Being a Christian isn't all that complicated. The very word "Christian" means "Christ-like." We are to simply be like Jesus, and, therefore, imitate God's standards. To do that, we must love as Jesus loved–the Father above all else, and others as He loves them and loves us.

_____

_____

_____

_____

_____

_____

_____

HITTING THE TARGET

Proverbs 13:20 (ESV)
Whoever walks with the wise becomes wise, but the companion of fools will suffer harm.

Our life is like an arrow flying through time. Somewhere out there is a target to shoot at, but an arrow flying without stability rarely hits the target.

What adds stability to the arrow shaft? It is generally three fletching or feathers. The three fletching in our lives should be;

- The scripture – we need to be continually reading God's word to gain the wisdom on how we get through life.
- The Spirit – when we've come to Christ we are given the Holy Spirit to fill us and direct us in right and wrong.
- The saints – surround yourself with the saints or Christians that will hold you accountable. They will lead you and keep you going straight.

So for true stability in life allow these three things to help you to hit the "life target" that God has set before you; the scripture in front of you, the Spirit inside you and the saints around you. Keep them all there, all the time and you will hit the target.

BROTHERS BUILDING BROTHERS

Psalms 133:1 (NKJV)
Behold, how good and how pleasant it is for brothers
to dwell together in unity!

There are few places that build strong relationships better than a hunting camp or a mountain. Some of the best friend/brotherly relationships were made and nurtured there. Once those brother to brother relationships are born it is so great to "dwell together in unity."

I've built some of my best friendships chasing elk, deer and turkeys around the mountains, plains and forests of the USA. Men of God have supported me because they know I support them. I can honestly say that I love these guys and I hold them up in their lives.

Relationships built with godly men are desperately needed in our world today. The pressures of standing alone will weaken or destroy many men. Seek out men of like mind and allow these friends to mold and support you.

Proverbs 27:17 (NIV) as iron sharpens iron, so one person sharpens another.

Allow those relationships to build and sharpen you.

JUST ASK

Matthew 7:7-8 (NIV)

"Ask and it will be given to you; seek and you will find; knock and the door will be opened to you. For everyone who asks receives; the one who seeks finds; and to the one who knocks, the door will be opened.

I wonder how many times in our lives we miss out on great opportunities or blessing, because we didn't ask. It is like being out turkey hunting, we can have pockets full of calls, slate calls, box calls, wingbone calls etc, but if we never take them out and call to the turkeys; our chances of getting an answer are non-existent.

God gives us the greatest gift of all, eternal life with Him. This is totally a gift and we have to do nothing, just let Him give it and accept it in faith. The other blessings in the life that are God given need to be asked for. As the verses say ASK, SEEK, KNOCK. Not hard to do, but an action is required.

Think of it like this... What a great pleasure it is when one of our kids or grand-kids crawls up into our laps and asks for something we can't wait to give them.

God has that same desire... To give us our deepest desires. All we have to do is ask.

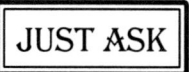

_____

_____

_____

_____

_____

_____

_____

_____

RUSTING OUT FROM INACTIVITY

1 Peter 4:10-11 (ESV)
As each has received a gift, use it to serve one another, as good stewards of God's varied grace: whoever speaks, as one who speaks oracles of God; whoever serves, as one who serves by the strength that God supplies—in order that in everything God may be glorified through Jesus Christ. To Him belong glory and dominion forever and ever. Amen.

T heodore Roosevelt once said, "Let us rather run the risk of wearing out than rusting out."

For many years I've hunted and guided around the western states. One thing that I have noticed in the prairies and mountains is in the past decades, people ran their vehicles until they just wouldn't go anymore. The vehicles were used until they had nothing left to give... then they were just left where they quit. They had nothing left to give. They owed their owners nothing at that point.

We all have been given gifts, some more visible than others. All are equally important in God's eyes. But they have no value at all if they are not put to use. Allowing your talents to sit idle is dangerous in that we can lose our ability to clearly see where and when it is valuable. We also stand the chance of having our gift pulled away. In Matthew 25 this is illustrated in a parable. The one servant that didn't use his talent lost it.

Put to use your God given gifts and talents... "Let us rather run the risk of wearing out than rusting out."

A good read Matthew 25:14-30

SOIL TYPES

Matthew 13:3-9 (NIV)
"...A farmer went out to sow his seed. 4 As he was scattering the seed, some fell along the path, and the birds came and ate it up. 5 Some fell on rocky places, where it did not have much soil. It sprang up quickly, because the soil was shallow. 6 But when the sun came up, the plants were scorched, and they withered because they had no root. 7 Other seed fell among thorns, which grew up and choked the plants. 8 Still other seed fell on good soil, where it produced a crop—a hundred, sixty or thirty times what was sown. 9 Whoever has ears, let them hear."

I lease a farm that where we hunt for deer each year. The farm has rolling fields and some wet swamps. The other day I checked a field, we call the slippery slope, located on the far back end of the farm. You can't see the field from anywhere else on the property so I was surprised to find the field had no crops planted and was all stones with very little soil exposed. The rest of the farm is growing great crops this year. It made me think of this passage.

Not only do we deal with rocky soils, but many times in our lives we allow things and circumstances to scorch what God is trying to do in and through us. We don't water and fertilize by times of prayer and scripture. We also deal with surrounding ourselves with "thorns," those people that intentionally or unintentionally choke out what God wants for us.

Whatever God plants in your life, water and care for it, remove the weeds from it and allow it to thrive. If you ever want to see growth or a harvest these things need to be done.

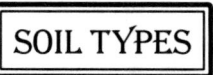

_____

_____

_____

_____

_____

_____

THE JOY OF AN ARROW IN FLIGHT

1 John 3:7-8 (NIV)

Dear children, do not let anyone lead you astray. The one who does what is right is righteous, just as he is righteous. 8 The one who does what is sinful is of the devil, because the devil has been sinning from the beginning. The reason the Son of God appeared was to destroy the devil's work.

I love old movies where they show archery in medieval times. One of the Robin Hood movies showed men being taught to shoot longbows. I enjoy scenes where an entire company of men release arrows at once toward oncoming combatants. The sight of arrows flying high through the air is something of beauty to me.

Several years ago a good friend, David, built a small bamboo longbow for Micah our grandson who was 3 at the time. It is beautiful with Osage orange and bamboo laminates and it shot like a dream for him, considering Micah's age. On the back of the bow David wrote these words, "may you never lose the joy of an arrow in flight."

Our lives are very much like the flight of an arrow. We need stability to hit the mark we are aiming for. The arrow has feathers or fletching to keep it stable. Without these feathers the arrow will fly off target after a short time. It might fly straight and true for a time, but it will very quickly lose its path.

Unless we spend time with God in His word and prayer, we are like a featherless arrow, sure to be off course.

Stabilize your flight in life; hold tight to God in prayer and in reading His word so you "never lose the joy of an arrow in flight."

PURE POWER

Jeremiah 10:13 (NIV)
When He thunders, the waters in the heavens roar; He makes clouds rise from the ends of the earth. He sends lightning with the rain and brings out the wind from His storehouses.

We have a tendency to always categorize God as love. We picture him as a "grandfather in the sky." What we tend to forget is God is ALL powerful!

I'm sitting this morning looking out the window, watching the flashes of lighting light up the trees in the yard. There's hail pounding on the metal roof and thunder shaking the house. He is a powerful force. I've seen His power in the swamps of Florida with the alligators and I've seen it in the mountains of Alaska with grizzly bears. His power amazes me, it is beyond my understanding.

Today is a great reminder that God has more power than our human minds can comprehend. The most amazing thing to me is that all of this amazing power is available to us 100% of the time; we just have to call on Him. He is our Father.

Romans 8:17 (KJV)
And if children, then heirs; heirs of God, and joint-heirs with Christ; if indeed we share in His sufferings so that we may be also glorified together.

LOOKING OUT FOR OTHERS

Philippians 2:3-4 (NIV)
Do nothing out of selfish ambition or vain conceit. Rather, in humility value others above yourselves, not looking to your own interests but each of you to the interests of the others.

I am not against putting anyone else first, but the thought of "never" doing anything out of selfish ambition, seems unreachable. However, if we really looked out for "the interests of the others," what a fantastic world it would be.

I've learned through a life of guiding that if you don't put others first it is hard to get ahead in life. If you were to take up a guiding lifestyle you would soon learn that living life this way is so rewarding. I've learned that to watch someone else succeed, at times, is more fulfilling than succeeding myself. I see this in my brother Dave as he guides elk hunters. He has lost the need to hunt for himself because he gives so much to put others first.

Selfish ambition and vain conceit verses humility and the interests of others. Not only would my world be better, but like Zig Ziglar wrote, "you can get whatever you want out of life by helping enough other people get what they want."

So by looking out for others first it gets me what I want/need in the long run? This sounds good; like a win/win to me. Besides it follows what we are commanded to do.

_____

_____

_____

_____

_____

_____

_____

CLEANING HOUSE

Luke 11:24-26 (NIV)

"When an impure spirit comes out of a person, it goes through arid places seeking rest and does not find it. Then it says, 'I will return to the house I left.' 25 When it arrives, it finds the house swept clean and put in order. 26 Then it goes and takes seven other spirits more wicked than itself, and they go in and live there. And the final condition of that person is worse than the first."

Throughout our lives we continually deal with temptation and sin. There are times that we fall into sin, but 1 John 1:9 says, "If we confess our sin, He is faithful and just to forgive us our sins and cleanse us from all unrighteousness."

Over the span of the last 20 years I have put many food plots in for hunting. When I first started tilling land I assumed that if I tilled the land and turned the weeds and grasses under, I would have fresh clean soil. But what I found was that if I didn't kill the weeds first and then plant something that would combat the weeds they would come back heavier and healthier. Just tilling and allowing the soil to lay never works as the weeds and grasses will take over very quickly.

The same is true of our life, once we've confessed and been forgiven we need to fill that space in our lives with more of God. If we don't fill that space with godly things, Satan will come in stronger than before and consume us.

Protect your heart. Keep your eyes on God and fill your life with godly things.

ON THE MOUNTAIN TOP

Mark 9:2-3 (NIV)
And after six days Jesus took with him Peter and James and John, and led them up a high mountain by themselves. And He was transfigured before them, and His clothes became radiant, intensely white, as no one on earth could bleach them.

All of us have had "mountain top" experiences in our Christian walk, times where the Lord has brought us to a place where we see Him more clearly and feel His presence. We come away wanting more of Him.

The other day I was in such a place both spiritually and physically. I had climbed up high looking for elk and was sitting on the rim of the Sangre de Christo Mountains looking over hundreds of miles of beauty. It was such a fulfilling place and time that I didn't want it to ever end. But eventually I had to come down to our hunting camp.

But as surely as we hit those mountain tops, we will also hit the valley floor. God lets us see those mountain tops so we know Him better. So we can best know His power, strength and love. That way when we hit the low spots in our lives we can remember how great our God is and hold on to Him.

Next time we hit the valley bottom remember that God has a plan to carry us to the top of the mountain again.

GOD'S TROPHY

Jude 1:24-25 (NASB)
Now to Him who is able to protect you from stumbling and to make you stand in the presence of His glory, blameless and with great joy, 25 to the only God our Savior, through Jesus Christ our Lord, be glory, majesty, power, and authority before all time, now, and forever. Amen.

As a kid we all love to put a trophy on the shelf of our bedroom or the family room mantle. It shows some sort of significant accomplishment in life. Then as hunters and fisherman we grow to hang mounts and photographs on the wall. These are not only accomplishments but also memories of time spent in the field with friends and family. Memories that will always a bring smile when we see that trophy.

Did you ever think that we are a trophy of God, or more accurately, a trophy of God's grace? Think about what God's grace is toward us. The most common definition of grace is, "God's unmerited favor." That is a great definition, but let's go a little further.

God's grace is to offer each and every one of us the gift of eternal life. He loved us enough to send His only Son, leaving heaven, to come to earth and die on our behalf. He did all this while not a single one of us deserved in any way at all. It was done totally independent of our own merit.

If you've accepted God's beautiful gift of grace think of your picture on God's wall. When He looks at it, He smiles knowing that you are His. If you haven't yet taken hold of that gift of a loving Father, do it now. Repent of your sins and put your faith in the Lord Jesus Christ. He died on the cross 2,000 years ago so you could be a recipient of God's grace. Receive the gift of Salvation and forever be a Trophy of God's Grace.

_____

_____

_____

_____

_____

CREATE IN ME A CLEAN HEART

Psalm 51:1-12 (NIV)

Have mercy on me, O God, according to your unfailing love; according to your great compassion blot out my transgressions. 2 Wash away all my iniquity and cleanse me from my sin. 3 For I know my transgressions, and my sin is always before me. 4 Against you, you only, have I sinned and done what is evil in your sight; so you are right in your verdict and justified when you judge. 5 Surely I was sinful at birth, sinful from the time my mother conceived me. 6 Yet you desired faithfulness even in the womb; you taught me wisdom in that secret place. 7 Cleanse me with hyssop, and I will be clean; wash me, and I will be whiter than snow. 8 Let me hear joy and gladness; let the bones you have crushed rejoice. 9 Hide your face from my sins and blot out all my iniquity. 10 Create in me a pure heart, O God, and renew a steadfast spirit within me. 11 Do not cast me from your presence or take your Holy Spirit from me. 12 Restore to me the joy of your salvation and grant me a willing spirit, to sustain me.

As a hunter, I put every effort to recover an animal when there has been a shot taken. I've spent days tracking, searching, walking and sometimes praying to try to find a wounded, or shot at, animal. And at times it has brought tears.

Considering that effort and emotion, how do I react when I've sinned? When I've drifted away from God's perfect plan for me? Do I lament over my actions like I do a misplaced or all together missed shot?

The scripture above was written by David when Nathan came to confront him about his sin of adultery. David was heartbroken over what he had done and he laid it all out before God.

We should consider David's response the next time we become aware of our sinful actions and lay ourselves right out and open before the Lord... Not just saying, "God I sinned, forgive me." But allow your sin (and more importantly God's forgiveness) to change you. "Create in me a pure heart, O God, and renew a steadfast spirit within me."

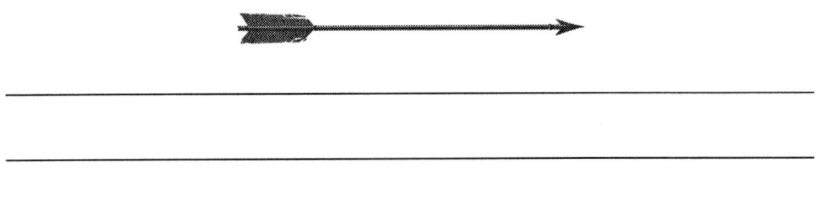

_____

_____

_____

KEEP GOING...

Hebrews 12:1 (NASB)
"Let us run with endurance the race that is set before us . . ."

H unting elk can be a terribly strenuous sport. Depending on the type of country that you hunt, it can actually be a dangerous endeavor. As I've guided in the Colorado mountains, I've had to continually tell myself or my hunter, "just a little further" or let's just "keep going" for bit more. Sometimes in my head I just hear, "keep going, keep going, keep going..." Without that continual prodding there would be little chance for success.

Many people have no idea how critical those two words are to success in life and in the Christian life. The biblical word is endurance or perseverance, the ability to keep on doing the things you have committed yourself to doing when you feel like it and when you don't feel like it. Nothing is more essential to success in the Christian life than perseverance. Faith gets you started; perseverance keeps you going.

Here's the question. What do you do when the pressure is on? It's easy to start the climb. All kinds of people come to the mountain, get up in the morning and put their hunting boots and start the climb. But when the miles click past and the muscles start to fatigue and life isn't easy anymore, what do they do? What do you do?

In James 1:2-3 (NLT), James tells us that we can look at the challenge to "keep going" with joy...

"My brothers, consider it pure joy when you fall into various trials knowing that the trying of your faith produces perseverance."

Staying power! Did you know that if God could get that one thing into your life, He could give you everything else? James 1 goes on to say in verse 4, "But let perseverance have its perfect work that you may be perfect and complete, lacking nothing!"

Perseverance. Finishing strong. Keep going.

_____

_____

_____

SPIRITUAL WIND VEINS

Isaiah 40:3 (NIV)
A voice of one calling: "In the wilderness prepare the way for the Lord; make straight in the desert a highway for our God.

Each spring we turkey hunt in Eastern Minnesota, as far eastern as possible, as we are on the bluffs looking straight down into the Mississippi River. Each year we make a stop at one place, it's a 20' high silver pole right on the edge of the bluff. On top of that pole is a crudely shaped metal fish that swivels with the wind.

This fish is really a very roughly built wind vein. While there is really nothing special about this fish, it's not attractive, it doesn't have any historical meaning that I know, but it is serving a mission. The only job that this fish has is to point toward the wind. The fisherman on the mighty Mississippi River below can look up on that bluff and see the wind direction.

The other day I was having dinner with some friends and explained that I believe that we only have one main purpose in this life. For those that have come to Christ, our main job is to point others toward the source of our power and the One that sets our direction, Jesus Christ.

If Christ didn't fully expect us to point others to Him, why wouldn't he take us home as soon as we accept His gift? Like John the Baptist who was only here to point others toward Christ and like the wind vein fish, our job is to point others to where our power comes.

We can do that in many ways and I feel if we are not doing it with our lives and our tongues, we are missing out on major blessings from God's own hand.

How are you doing today? Are others seeing a Christ they can't live without because of your life and your testimony? Is the wind vein of your life continually pointing to Him; the one that gives us our power and direction? If not, check your life and make sure that you are lined up with the power that is supplied by Jesus!

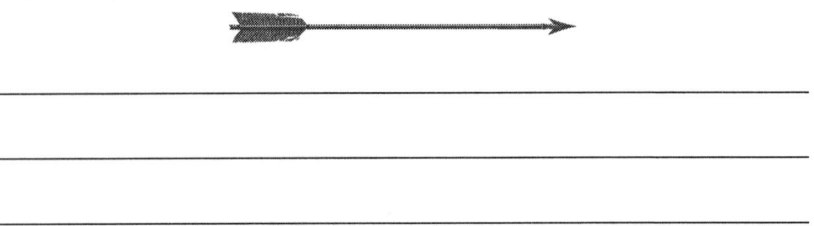

_____

_____

_____

IT'S NOT A PASSION, IT'S AN OBSESSION

Luke 24:32 (NIV)
They asked each other, "Were not our hearts burning within us while he talked with us on the road and opened the Scriptures to us?"

For those of you hunters reading this today you know that Mossy Oak Camouflage is the number one selling camo pattern in the country. Some of you have heard Toxey Haas, the owner and originator of Mossy Oak say that, "it all began with a fistful of dirt." Toxey believes, as I do, that God showed him that from that fistful of dirt, along with the leaves and sticks mixed in, he could make a camouflage pattern that would be like no other.

Mossy Oak's motto says, "It's not a passion, it's an obsession." They are talking about hunting and their obsession for making good camouflage. But it hit me that this is the way my spiritual life should be. If God truly is my creator and He truly sent His Son to die for me... How could I not be obsessed with Him and His love for me?

What is an obsession? Obsession has been defined this way; an idea or thought that continually preoccupies or intrudes on a person's mind. As in, "he was in the grip of an obsession he was powerless to resist."

That's what we should each want for our lives, an obsession for God that we are "powerless to resist." When our thoughts of godly things are continually preoccupying and intruding on our everyday life.

Not many of us have known true hunger or thirst. We might have been a little uncomfortable concerning something to eat or drink... But a true desperate need for food or drink is how I should desire God and His word.

I hope that for you and me, He will become your obsession not just your passion.

NEEDED NUTRITION

1 Peter 2:2 (NIV)
Like newborn babies, crave pure spiritual milk, so that by it you may grow up in your salvation.

The past few days I've been busy putting out mineral for the deer on my leases. We've seen some dramatic differences in the deer when they have an intake of the nutrition that they need. We've planted food plots, supplement the feed and have mineral stations where we've used Mossy Oak's Biologic, Bio-Rocks to help boost the nutrition, health and strength of our local deer herd.

People are like deer, if we don't get the right physical nutrition we become weak and ineffective. More importantly, if we don't get the right spiritual nutrition we don't grow or stay healthy and strong.

Spiritual health comes from a few things; consistent reading and study of God's word, a strong prayer time with Him and being surrounded by other members of God's family. Without these three things we can survive but we can't thrive. When we get infected by the worldly influences around us we fall subject to weakness... Just like we would with a cold or the flue.

So build up your spiritual immunity, read daily, pray constantly and keep in close contact with those that expect the best and most from you. If you do these things you will continue to be strong and have a healthy spiritual life.

Joshua 1:8 (NIV)
Keep this Book of the Law always on your lips; meditate on it day and night, so that you may be careful to do everything written in it. Then you will be prosperous and successful.

SLOW DOWN... SEE BEYOND

Luke 12:27

"Consider how the wild flowers grow. They do not labor or spin. Yet I tell you, not even Solomon in all his splendor was dressed like one of these."

G od's creation is an amazing thing. When we look around at the beauty of nature in its entire splendor, a small wildflower, a crystal stream, a floating eagle on the afternoon thermals, a deer browsing on summer growth, how can someone look around and say, there is no Creator? Yet, so many of us see this all with our eyes daily and it rarely gets to our hearts.

Being an avid outdoorsman, I love to see game animals and have probably been guilty of looking past the beauty of the big picture to see something else. To see a bull elk is a fantastic sight, but if we miss the golden aspens, the seeping springs, the magpie or the mountain... We may have missed the best parts of creation.

Slow down, release the "pinpoint focuses" of life and learn to appreciate the whole picture. Slow down, breath in deep and appreciate the breath. Slow down, and learn to see all that God has to bless you.

Lao Tzu gave good advice with one small quote. "Nature does not hurry, yet everything is accomplished."

Learn to see beyond your focus of this moment. God has so much for us to see and appreciate.

PRACTICE, PRACTICE, PRACTICE!

1 Samuel 16:7

But the Lord said to Samuel, "Do not consider his appearance or his height, for I have rejected him. The Lord does not look at the things people look at. People look at the outward appearance, but the Lord looks at the heart."

God has given me an eye for things in nature... I've been very blessed with the ability to see things that are out of place, things that just don't belong. One time I was driving down a gravel road on Kodiak Island and something caught my eye way off in the woods. I backed up (no traffic on the roads there) and walked back into the woods. Way back in there was a world class antler from a blacktail deer.

I can't take any credit for that ability, God blessed me with it. But the more we use the gifts that we are blessed with the keener they become. Discernment is a gift that God gives all His children, but if we don't use it and practice it regularly it doesn't become sharp.

There are so many false teachings and teachers in our world today...Things that are so close to the truth, yet fall short. We have to measure everything against the word of God... If it seems, "not quite right" study it further.

In Romans 12:2 Paul explained to the Romans... "And do not be conformed to this world, but be transformed by the renewing of your mind, so that you may prove what the will of God is, that which is good and acceptable and perfect."

Our hearts become renewed when we put our trust in Christ. Our minds are continually being renewed by godly living, actions and thoughts.

_____

_____

_____

_____

_____

_____

A GOOD TURKEY HUNTER

James 1:14-15

... but each person is tempted when they are dragged away by their own evil desire and enticed. 15 Then, after desire has conceived, it gives birth to sin; and sin, when it is full-grown, gives birth to death.

I've been a turkey hunter for over 30 years and I hope that over that time I've gotten better at the fundamentals and art of turkey hunting. Anyone, if they sit long enough in the turkey woods can eventually kill a turkey. But a good turkey hunter perfects the talents that it takes to be consistently successful.

Satan would make a good turkey hunter, really. To be a good turkey hunter you have to be somewhat cunning, thinking like a turkey and planning your next move. You have to be deceptive with the use of calls and decoys at times. Lastly to harvest a turkey you have to be willing to pull the trigger and kill it.

Consider Genesis 3:1-7 we can read the story of how man fell into sin. We can see how Satan offered a lie (the call), how Eve looked at the fruit (the decoy) and how they fell and lost everything (death). It sounds like a turkey hunt, doesn't it?

The difference between a good turkey hunter and Satan is this, a good turkey hunter doesn't kill all of the turkeys he comes in contact with, he is selective and he had a respect for his quarry... Satan has no respect for any life and he strives to kill every person he can.

1 Peter 5:8 "Be alert and of sober mind. Your enemy, the devil, prowls around like a roaring lion looking for someone to devour."

There is no better killer than a cat and the king of the cats is the lion. Satan is like a cunning cat seeking to kill and devour you. Don't fall for his calls or decoys, stay out of range and protect yourself by surrounding yourself with godly people and things.

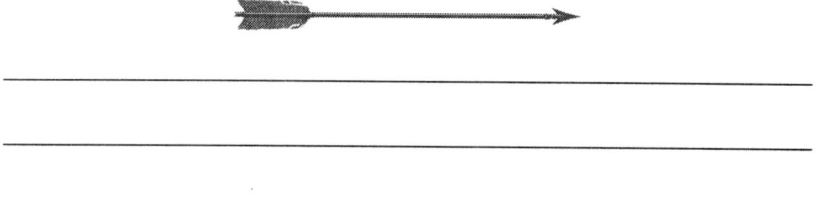

_____

_____

_____

QUIT LIVING MEMORIES

Philippians 3:13-14
Brothers and sisters, I do not consider myself yet to have taken hold of it. But one thing I do: Forgetting what is behind and straining toward what is ahead, 14 I press on toward the goal to win the prize for which God has called me heavenward in Christ Jesus.

There is a saying in hunting that goes, "you are hunting memories." This means that you are spending your time hunting places that produced years ago, but things have changed and the animals just aren't there anymore. A hunter doing this usually gets discouraged and it is very unproductive.

The same can be true of our lives, aside from hunting. So many of us allow our past to drag us down and to waste so much of life. This is a trap of Satan, don't fall into it. Satan wants us to dwell on the sin and shame of our past and that will continue to makes us unproductive in what God has called us to do. But just like "hunting memories" it will discourage us and make our walk unproductive.

When the apostle Paul wrote this he knew that if he "lived in his past" He could not be productive because the guilt would bring him down. Paul hunted down and killed Christians... How bad is your past? I bet it isn't that bad.

Psalm 103:12 As far as the east is from the west, so far hath he removed our transgressions/sins from us.

If God has removed your sins, let them go, quit living memories.

ACKNOWLEDGE HIM

Proverbs 16:9 (KJV)
A man's heart deviseth his way: but the Lord directeth his steps.

As a hunting guide we take on heavy responsibility at times. I have had hunts where I have searched at midnight for a lost hunter with temperatures well below zero. I've had to find my way out of dark woods miles from nowhere to save my hunter and myself from an uncomfortable night outdoors. And, I've brought a boat full of hunters across 15 miles of northern Canadian lakes at midnight. I know of hunters who have had their lives saved by a guide while hunting dangerous game. What would have become of those very people if it hadn't been for a guide? They would have wandered around aimlessly hoping to find their way in the darkness. Worst case, they might have died for not knowing how to get out of their situation.

God is our ultimate guide... We can plan and prepare for situations in life but in the end, God will direct us to where we need to be. So often we wander through life when we have the best guide available at a moment's notice. Allow Him to hold your hand in the darkness, to carry your load when it gets too heavy. Just allow God to direct your path. We just have to "acknowledge Him."

Proverbs 3:6 In all your ways acknowledge Him, and He shall direct your paths.

_____

_____

_____

_____

_____

_____

_____

_____

THE LEGACY WE LEAVE

John 17:1
"Father, the hour has come. Glorify your Son, that your Son may glorify you"

Yesterday, while walking on the mountain, I came across several quaking aspen trees that bears had climbed many years ago. The aspens show the claw marks where the bear gripped for climbing. Some of these trees were nearly 100' in height and probably 100 years old. The thought came to me that the impression of the bear's claws were left for many generations to see. Then it came to me, all the "marks" that I leave in life will also be seen for generations to come. I find it significant in John 17:1 even the Son did not seek glory for Himself, but to glorify the Father. Jesus didn't want any credit; He wanted to point it all to the father. He just wanted to be obedient to His calling.

So what will your legacy be? We can build a building. We can plant a church. We can strive to be remembered for all kinds of good things... But what does God desire our legacy to be? It's obedience, pure and simple obedience.
Now that's a legacy worth living out. Not a building or an institution, but living men and women who carry on His mission for His glory. I cannot do this by myself, but I can focus my obedience so that Christ impacts others and they choose to live for Him. There is no glory for me, of course, but there is great glory for Him because only He can do this through me.

Leave your mark for generations to come. It is the LEGACY WE LEAVE

MOVE FORWARD

Luke 14:28 (ESV)
28 For which of you, desiring to build a tower, does not first sit down and count the cost, whether he has enough to complete it?.

I love to plan a hunting trip. I'll have maps, atlases, aerial photos, lists, lists and more lists scattered all over months before the departure date. To plan a Western elk hunt I will watch elk hunting videos to mentally prepare myself for the hunt. I want to visualize me taking an elk or if I'm guiding, my hunter getting one. A positive attitude and planning ahead for every possible obstacle is what it takes to be successful. We can plan and be successful or we can fail to plan and look back and wish we had.

Someone once said, that "the best time to plant a tree is twenty years ago and today."

Think about that for a minute or two. Then answer these questions. In ten years, what will you wish you started today? What will you wish you had planned for?

In 10 years, where do you want to be as a person? As a Christian? What do you want God to accomplish through you and in your life? Write it down and start planning. Don't wait for 10 years and wish you had done it. Set your heart on what God wants of you and move forward.

Jeremiah 29:11 tells us...
11 For I know the thoughts that I think toward you, says the Lord, thoughts of peace and not of evil, to give you a future and a hope.

God has a plan for you. He wants you to succeed. All you have to do is look for His plan, read His word, talk to Him, surround yourself with His people and start moving forward. God will bless your work if you make your plans based on His word and His plans for you.

Move forward.

_____

_____

_____

WHERE'S YOUR ANCHOR?

Psalm 62:1-2 (NIV)
Truly my soul finds rest in God; my salvation comes from him. 2 Truly he is my rock and my salvation; he is my fortress, I will never be shaken.

The radio in the lodge was calling my name and when I picked up, the voice on the other end said, "Dean, one of your boat captains is calling mayday out on 7 mile Beach. He is going down." Even as I write this it still bring a sick feeling in my gut.

Our fishing boat along with its captains and five guests was stuck on a shoal on the deadliest stretch of sea around North America, the Shelikof Strait. Captain Hugh jumped off the boat's bow, taking the anchor rope and anchor to shore. Once he got to shore he sunk the anchor into the sand and the five guests were able to get to shore. Without that anchor the heavy waves and quick rising tides that engulfed the 26 ft boat, may very well have claimed the life of the young boys and elderly gentleman on board that day.

In our daily lives, Christ should be that anchor. When the storms of life pound on us and it feels like there is no way to get to shore, Christ is what saves us. We need to allow Him to hold us and protect us from being pounded on.

No doubt the storms will come and no doubt that we will be tossed around by the waves of trouble in life. But if we allow Christ to be our anchor we can withstand any storm.

All guests and the captain made it safely to shore that day and we were able to save all of them. If it hadn't been for a strong immovable anchor, it might not have ended well.

Where's your anchor?

Ray Boltz recorded the song The Anchor Holds about just this. The chorus goes...

The anchor holds
Though the ship is battered
The anchor holds
Though the sails are torn

Allow your anchor to hold you.

NOT OF WORKS

Ephesians 2:8-9
For it is by grace that you have been saved, through faith, not of works,
it is a gift of God so that no one may boast.

I've read these verses 1,000 times and memorized them as a young boy... And

I totally believe it. But, do I live it out in my daily life? As hunters, we've learned that there are no "sure things." We believe that we have a buck located and patterned or a gobbler roosted and we figure this is going to be a slam dunk. However, we can't control the weather, the animal or God's will.

In the end we go out hunting with the faith that our part is done. The same is true of Salvation, our part is to have faith and accept God's gift. The rest is up to Him.

I can live out the "saved by grace, through faith" part. It's the "not of works" part that I mess up all the time. I allow Satan to convince me that I have to keep earning God's love. I forget that Christ died once for all.

1John 1:9 tells us that, "if we confess our sins He is faithful and just to forgive our sins and cleanse us from ALL unrighteousness." Not some of our unrighteousness but ALL of it! We can stop trying to earn God's favor; Christ paid the price for that on the cross.

We need to learn to live free.

_____

_____

_____

_____

_____

_____

GIVE ME STRENGTH

Isaiah 40:29
He gives strength to the weary and increases power to the weak.

A few years ago I went for a long hike in the woods with a couple of friends. It was mid July and we started early in the morning and the weather was warm but we didn't think much of it. By late morning the weather had turned very hot and we realized we hadn't brought any water with us. I was in trouble.

Just before noon we crossed a small stream on top of a log. I fell as I got to the far side and when I went down I got an abdominal cramp. When I tried to get up I got cramps in both legs and arms as well as most of the rest of my body... I was totally immobilized. We had to radio for someone to bring water to us in the middle of that swamp. If I had been alone without a radio, I probably would have died as I was so dehydrated.

Like the story of the "Woman at the Well" that water brought me life... But it was a temporary life. My physical body is dying, we all are. But Jesus gives us an amazing strength, the power over not only death when we leave this world, but also power over demonic forces in this world.

Like the water that revitalized my strength, Jesus can lift us when we are struggling to take even one more step, make one more small move in life. He can be all we need to push us through when we need just a little more.

The great evangelist D.L. Moody once said,

"When a man has no strength, if he leans on God, he becomes powerful."

When we have nothing left to give, cry out to God, He is the giver of strength.

ABOUT THE AUTHOR
DEAN HULCE

There is no place like a campfire to tell hunting stories and Dean excels at storytelling. His experiences while hunting, fishing and guiding all across North America have given him an endless supply of material for his writing and speaking engagements. From the Mountain tops of Alaska to the Rio Grande River Valley of Texas, the successes, the failures and near death experiences have added to the depth of his relationship with God.

Dean has written for several National magazines such as; Buckmasters, Rack, Safari, Safari Times, Whitetails, Christian Bowhunters of America and more. In addition, he has been writing a daily devotional for several years, many of them based on his hunting and outdoor experiences.

Along with his family, Dean has been fortunate to hunt many states and Canadian provinces for deer, bear, turkeys, bison, alligators and many others species.

Dean speaks on a regular basis at many outdoor events each year. He continues to write devotionals and is also producing Christian hunting videos. This is his second book, TROPHIES OF GRACE has been a huge success. Living the Dream!

Allow Dean to take you on these adventures while learning what God wants us to learn from His Word.

CPSIA information can be obtained
at www.ICGtesting.com
Printed in the USA
FFOW05n0846191116